More Rip-Roaring Reads
for Reluctant Teen Readers

More Rip-Roaring Reads
for Reluctant Teen Readers

Bette D. Ammon

Gale W. Sherman

1999
Libraries Unlimited, Inc.
Englewood, Colorado

*For Steve Sherman and Randy Ammon: patient, supportive,
and helpful . . . rip-roaring husbands!*

*Thanks to Stan Steiner, Harriet Whittelsey, Jill Walton, Nancy Spaulding, and
Ashley Sherman for assistance and advice.*

Libraries Unlimited, Inc.
P.O. Box 6633
Englewood, CO 80155-6633
1-800-237-6124
www.lu.com

Production Editor: Stephen Haenel
Assistant Editor: Felicity Tucker
Copy Editor: Melissa R. Root
Proofreader: Jason Cook
Typesetter: Michael Florman

Library of Congress Cataloging-in-Publication Data

Ammon, Bette DeBruyne.
   More rip-roaring reads for reluctant teen readers / Bette D. Ammon
and Gale W. Sherman.
    xii, 161 p. 22x28 cm.
    Sherman's name appears first in the earlier edition.
    Includes bibliographical references and indexes.
    ISBN 1-56308-571-2 (softbound)
    1. Young adult literature, American--Bibliography. 2. Teenagers--
United States--Books and reading. I. Sherman, Gale W. II. Title.
Z1037.S524 1998
[PS490]
016.8108'09283--dc21
                                 98-37150
                                     CIP

The book you gave me is way too long.
The print is too small
And I don't understand some of the longer words.
The story is boring.
I don't care if she refuses his love for two hundred
pages.
If he's so horny let him find someone else.
I don't care if she has to wear an A on her chest.
Everyone fools around these days.
I don't care if the daughter is illegitimate.
Nobody cares about that anymore.
Reading is like swimming through molasses, man.
Where's the rape? The murder? The action?
I gotta go, man.
The teacher's showing a video in my next class.

From *Who Killed Mr. Chippendale? A Mystery in Poems* by Mel Glenn (Lodestar Books, 1996), page 63. Copyright 1996 by Mel Glenn. Used by permission of Lodestar Books, an affiliate of Dutton Children's Books, a division of Penguin USA, Inc.

Contents

Introduction

For many teenagers, "Reading *is* like swimming through molasses," and most parents, teachers, and librarians are eager and willing to transform this experience. In Mel Glenn's poem, high school student P. J. Compson represents scores of reluctant readers—those who can read but choose not to for a variety of reasons. These aliterate individuals pose a particular challenge for educators who know that passing on the reading "bug" is critically important. Books have to be really special to capture a reluctant reader's attention.

Literacy among young people is a serious issue. Research indicates that up to fifty percent of third and fourth graders are reading below grade level, and many of these children will stop reading altogether by the time they reach middle school. We know that skill in reading is essential for success in school and in life. Also, we know that for readers, books offer a world of magic, information, and ongoing learning.

So, how do we "sell" this rapture to reluctant readers? How do we convince them that reading is not only fundamental but fun, meaningful, and well worth the investment of time and energy? The competition is fierce. Can we make books seem better than (or at least equal to) videos, interactive computer games, television, and the Internet?

The answer is a resounding YES! We begin by introducing nonreaders to exciting books that are impossible to put down. We offer students a choice—a variety of alternatives—fiction, nonfiction, adventure, mystery, the supernatural, and more. Reading accountability is not a dreaded chore. We allow and encourage consequential and interesting activities, related in some manner to the book and the student's life and concerns. We keep readers reading with ongoing lists of books related to student interest. We start with *More Rip-Roaring Reads for Reluctant Teen Readers*, which offers forty suggested titles plus a mountain of other information.

The purpose of this book (and its predecessor, *Rip-Roaring Reads for Reluctant Teen Readers*, 1993) is to bring together books and readers. By selecting forty contemporary, spellbinding books written by forty outstanding authors, we hope to make the matching process between student and book easier and more successful. Included are twenty rip-roaring reads for middle schoolers (grades 5 through 8) and twenty rip-roaring reads for high school students (grades 9 through 12). Interest and reading levels vary within each list, and many teachers, parents, and librarians will find books from both lists appropriate for their individual student or class. (Note: The selected titles are highly recommended for all readers, not just reluctant readers.)

Deciding upon these forty titles was a particularly difficult task, and because no one list pleases everybody all of the time, it is inevitable that a "favorite" title has been omitted. Currently, the abundance of reading material for children is remarkable and overwhelming, and recommended lists are ever-changing. In order to be included in *More Rip-Roaring Reads*, the books had to have the following characteristics:

1. Recent publication date. Just like adult readers, young adults are attracted to new materials. Older "mustn't miss" titles for teen readers are included as further reading suggestions (see bookmark explanations on p. xii).

2. Relatively short book length, preferably less than 150 and not more than 175 pages, because thick books are sometimes daunting. We kept in mind, however, that "thinness" is not necessarily an overriding criterion. Research shows that a highly motivated reader may be able to jump ahead at least two years in his or her reading level.

3. Appealing format. Typeface and font size are attractive with consideration given to page layout, paragraph length, amount of dialogue, and an attention-grabbing beginning. We avoided books with the traditional high/low look—a stigmatizing format with too-large print, poor-quality illustrations, overly wide margins, and so forth. Many of the books selected are available in paperback, which many teens prefer.

4. Eye-catching book jacket or cover with characters' ages accurately reflected.

5. High-interest, meaningful subject matters. Issues covered are topical, relevant, and captivating.

6. Appropriate reading levels. Most of the books selected were calculated at reading levels between fourth and seventh grade. Again, remember that high interest will frequently attract and motivate a reader even though the text may be somewhat difficult.

7. Notable authors. Many of the authors selected are current teen favorites and are regularly included on recommended lists.

8. Excellent writing, vivid and realistic characters, authentic dialogue, and gripping plots.

Using This Book

The layout of the forty book entries allows the reader to scan the information quickly, to view the books from various perspectives, and to consider using the work in a variety of ways. The bibliographic data that begin each entry are not only useful for ordering but contain other valuable information, such as the number of pages.

If the book is available in an audio version, that information is included. Books on audiocassette, compact disc, or video cannot replace reading experiences but can certainly capture interest and provide contact with authors and stories.

Genres and Themes

Just as teens have favorite musicians and television shows, they also have distinct preferences when it comes to material they will consider reading. Therefore, the genre selections for both age divisions are balanced and varied to help successfully match students with books. Popular genres such as contemporary realistic fiction, mystery, and adventure are included, but so are biographies, informational books, and graphic novels. Every reader (reluctant or not) can find something rip-roaring to read.

Books fit into specific genres because of certain literary characteristics, whereas themes unify the plot, setting, and characters. More often than not, most stories can be categorized into two or more genres and have multiple underlying themes. Multiple genre and theme notations encourage looking at each book from as wide a perspective as possible. This increases the opportunities for use in the classroom as well as the opportunities for matching books with potential readers. Themes for each title are listed in order of importance.

Readability and Interest Levels

Because readability evaluations are subjective, results often vary. Two separate readability factors were calculated for each book using the Fry Readability Scale. The results give approximate reading levels that need to be viewed in conjunction with the book's content, language style, and interest value.

Interest and readability levels frequently do not match. These rip-roaring reads were selected because they combined low readability levels with high interest levels. However, titles should not necessarily be dismissed if the reading level appears too high for your student or class. These may be perfect books to read aloud.

Choices should not be limited. Even poor readers will attempt to read material above their reading levels if they are intensely interested in the subject. Also, there is a fine line between providing books that are easy and those that are too easy, and therefore insulting. The more challenging book may be *the* book that changes a student from a reluctant reader to a ravenous reader.

Reviews

Citations are listed for reviews appearing in the major journals that evaluate children's literature and are the professional periodicals most readily accessible to librarians and teachers. These are *The Book Report*, *Booklist*, *Bulletin of the Center for Children's Books*, *Horn Book*, *Publishers Weekly*, *Kliatt Paperback and Audio Book Guide*, *School Library Journal*, and *Voice of Youth Advocates* (*VOYA*).

The differing viewpoints expressed by reviewers often provide diverse opinions about the same work. If a book was starred or recommended in these journal reviews, that information is included. These ratings are self-explanatory except for *VOYA*. The books reviewed in *VOYA* are rated for quality and popularity. They range from #1 ("Hard to understand how it got published" and "No young adult will read unless forced to for assignments") to #5 ("Hard to imagine it being better written" and "Every young adult [who reads] was dying to read it yesterday"). In addition, *VOYA* publishes reviews from teens as well as librarians and teachers.

Author Information

Many students are intrigued by details about authors' lives. For instance, a reluctant reader who is intrigued by aliens will love William Sleator's claim that "They" made him write his abduction adventure, *The Night the Heads Came*. And nonathletes who are avid sports fans will appreciate Dan Gutman's confession that he writes about sports even though he is a "terrible athlete" himself. If specific biographical information about the writing of any of these books was available, it is included.

Some authors have Internet home pages or e-mail addresses and want to correspond with readers. If those are available, they are provided here.

Plot Summary

Plot details are kept to a minimum. However, because most students prefer books with protagonists their own age or slightly older, the ages of the main characters are always stated or implied. Keep in mind that many teenagers prefer nonfiction books that may have no characters at all. Additional plot, setting, and character information can be gleaned from the themes, reviews, booktalks, and literature extensions/alternative book reports notations.

Introducing the Book

The hints in this section are intended to aid adults in sharing these books with individuals or groups of students. Some of the titles are good read-aloud candidates, and obviously they are all good selections for independent reading by both reluctant and avid teen readers. We often recommend reading aloud a particular passage or specific chapter and note that in this section. These selections, ranging from a few paragraphs to twelve or fifteen pages, are singled out to grab the interest of potential readers.

Some books are not appropriate to read aloud because of sensitive and personal subject matter, whereas others are especially suited to share at certain times of the year (Women's History Month) or within particular curricula (Civil War studies). This information is also included in this section.

Booktalks

Booktalking is a terrific way to sell books to potential readers. These talks should catch the listeners' attention the way "coming attractions" do at the movies. They are short and sweet and not the same as critical book reviews, reports, or analyses. The "On the Spot" booktalks are spontaneous sells, suitable for use when grabbing a book off the shelf or doing many quick booktalks together. Tantalizing information is given, but few specific details are included. "On the Spot" booktalks can be printed onto bookmarks and placed in the matching book.

Using excerpts from the text is the best way to give the true flavor of a book in a more prepared or traditional booktalk. "With the Author's Words" are booktalks that include a high-interest, quoted section from the book. When students see you read a selection from a book, they receive the nonverbal message that reading is pleasurable and that the pleasure comes from the book. Expect to sell books when booktalking! Do not disappoint students by not having the books available when you are finished. The canned, brief booktalks in *More Rip-Roaring Reads* may be used in presentations or duplicated and used in book displays or on bulletin boards.

Literature Extensions/Alternative Book Report Activities

The use of whole language and literature-based curricula makes using "real" books an integral and welcome part of classroom activities. But, please, forget the dreaded boring book report as an accountability method. Instead, encourage students to look at alternative activities such as the ones listed in this book. Do not, however, think of these ideas as the only ones! Use these as a springboard to help you, your colleagues, *and* your students formulate other activities.

Another suggestion is to approach reading accountability backwards. Students can take a look at the alternative ideas and select a book to read based on an activity that holds interest for them.

As use of the Internet and all its treasures becomes more and more a part of our lives, it is logical to link reading projects to appropriate sites on the World Wide Web. We have provided numerous suggestions, all up and running when accessed August 1, 1998.

Do not be discouraged if your library does not have all the books recommended for further research and reading. In this day of limited budgets, no library will have them all, and that is why numerous choices are listed. To expand your materials collection, use interlibrary loan services that most public libraries offer. Remember, unless a student is particularly interested in a specific project, they should not be spending more time on the activity than they did reading the book!

Bookmarks

Because the primary reason for *More Rip-Roaring Reads* is to create lifelong readers, we want students to ask for more when they finish reading a book. These reproducible bookmarks will help match books with readers at a variety of reading levels and, most important, hook them on books and keep them reading.

Each list includes books that extend reading experiences by listing other books by that particular author or by listing other outstanding titles in a particular genre, theme, series, or topic area. The bookmarks include appropriate books for all readers at a variety of reading levels.

Adapt these to your own individual needs. Add additional titles from your library and mark the titles you have in your collection or the titles available from another library in your area. These bookmarks do not need to be used only in connection with each specific entry. Each entry in this book has been listed on its appropriate bookmark, so you can use them anytime for all kinds of readers!

Indexes

There are two indexes in this book. The first index cross-references every title and author listed throughout the book. Forty different books and authors are featured in the main entries, but more than 1,500 additional titles and authors are also listed in the literature extensions, alternative book report activities, or on the 120 bookmarks.

The second index combines genres, themes, and extension activities. These indexes help librarians, teachers, and other adults make connections with books and assist them in matching readers with appropriate materials.

✳✳✳

Popular young adult mystery writer Joan Lowery Nixon says that she often receives letters from students who had never completed an entire book before they cruised through one of her mysteries. One ninth-grade girl wrote that she had always hated reading until she read one of Nixon's books. She wrote to Nixon: "Thank you for the gift of reading."

Good luck with your endeavors. Just one person can make a difference in a reluctant reader's life and give that gift of reading. Maybe that person is you. When book and reader meet, anything is possible. So, introduce a few!

More Rip-Roaring Reads
for Middle School Students

Balgassi, Haemi

Tae's Sonata

LC 96-29081. 1997. 128p. $14.00 (ISBN 0-395-84314-6). Clarion Books.

Genres: Contemporary realistic fiction, romance, multicultural

Themes: Korean Americans, friendship, school life, family life, acceptance, cliques, prejudice, racism, vandals, immigrants, homesickness, cultures, heritage, music—piano, crushes, boy-girl relationships, cruelty, rumors, reports, compassion, peer relationships

Reading level: Fifth grade

Interest level: Sixth through ninth grade

Reviews:
Booklist. 94(4):404 October 15, 1997.
Bulletin of the Center for Children's Books. 51(3):80 November 1997. (Recommended)
Publishers Weekly. 244(26):76 June 30, 1997.
School Library Journal. 43(9):210 September 1997.

Author Information

Haemi Balgassi was born in South Korea and immigrated to the United States when she was seven. She knew from age nine that she wanted to be a writer and began her career in her mid-twenties. She tries to write some every day, but when she gets caught up in a story she writes for stretches as long as twenty hours. This happened when she began *Tae's Sonata* on January 1, 1996; she finished the book on January 31. Readers can send Balgassi e-mail at peacebound@juno.com and visit her Website at http://home.sprynet.com/sprynet/balgassi/, through which she has met children "online from all over the world." Balgassi lives with her husband and daughter in the city she grew up in—Westfield, Massachusetts.

Plot Summary

Not only is eighth-grader Taeyoung Kim struggling to fit in with her peers, she is also striving to reconcile her Korean heritage with her new American culture. When popular Josh Morgan chooses Tae as a partner for a history project about South Korea, she wonders if he is just using her to improve his grade.

Introducing the Book

The short length and lower reading level of this book make it ideal for independent reading. Because the tension of the story starts immediately, reading aloud the first chapter will grab the attention of potential readers.

Booktalks

On the Spot

Tae feels out of place and just wants to blend in with her American classmates. Being assigned South Korea (her country of birth) for her geography project isn't going to help. Potential boyfriends and rumors make Tae's life even more complicated!

With the Author's Words

Tae is almost asleep when she hears her mother ask,

> *"Taeyoung? Are you happy we moved here?". . . I keep my eyes closed, even though I'm wide awake now. A part of me wants to cry out that no, I'm not glad. I want to tell her how much I miss our old house in Seoul . . . how much I want to run through the field of wild cosmos where my friends and I used to play . . . how I ache for the school where I fit in without ever having to try. (pp. 82–83)*

Tae's fears about eighth grade and making friends are pretty typical, but her struggle is harder because she's torn between her Korean heritage and the appeal of American ways. Read *Tae's Sonata* to find out how her conflict is resolved.

Literature Extensions/Alternative Book Report Activities

Social Issues/Current Events/Human Rights/Racial Conflict/Korean Americans—Tae's parents remove the hardened egg yolk from their store sign in quiet defiance of the racist action. Eve Bunting's picture book *Smoky Night* (Harcourt, Brace & Company, 1994), illustrated by David Diaz, is based on the Los Angeles riots of 1992 and also features racial tension between Korean American merchants and other minorities. The simmering hostilities between many Korean immigrant merchants and other minority groups, especially impoverished customers, has been the focus of racial conflicts in many of our country's inner cities.

Students can find out more about this topic, including specific information about boycotts of Korean-owned grocery stores. Invite a representative from your local human rights group to speak about this and other related topics. How do students think they can help protect each other's rights and existence? Are there opportunities for students to become involved locally?

Social Skills/Self-Esteem—Regardless of culture or ethnic origin, many middle school students are like Tae and need assistance developing social skills and dealing with the roller coaster aspects of adolescence. Provide students with the following self-help books: *Straight Up!: A Teenager's Guide to Taking Charge of Your Life* by Elizabeth Taylor-Gerdes and Cortrell J. Harris (Lindsey Publishing, 1995); *Finding Our Way: The Teen Girls' Survival Guide* by Allison Abner and Linda Villarosa (HarperPerennial Library, 1996); *Bodypride: An Action Plan for Teens: Seeking Self-Esteem and Building Better Bodies* by Cynthia Stamper Graff, et al. (Griffin Publishers, 1997); *How to Survive As a Teen: When No One Understands* by Stevan E. Atanasoff (Herald, 1989); and *Smart Moves: How to Succeed in School, Sports, Career, and Life* by Dick DeVenzio (Prometheus Books, 1989).

Social Studies/Countries/South Korea/Internet—Students can do more interesting studies about countries than the written report Tae and Josh produced. More active learning could include the following: 1) Interviewing first-generation immigrants like Tae's parents to collect firsthand information; 2) preparing and sampling traditional foods (kimchee, fried mondu, rice, sweet potato fritters, fried tofu, and spicy bean sprout soup would be appropriate food for a study of Korea); 3) visiting major Internet sites for the selected country. Students studying Korea may begin by looking at "Korea.com" at http://www.korea.com/ and "Korea Info" at http://204.94.70.10/korea/korea.htm.

Social Studies/Immigration—Balgassi writes convincingly about immigrants who often struggle to balance and maintain their traditions alongside an overwhelming American culture. Min Paek's *Aekyung's Dream* (Children's Book Press, 1988) also features a young Korean immigrant learning to adapt to her new American life. Various members of these families respond differently, but typical problems include dealing with isolation, homesickness, language barriers, acceptance, and the like.

Most studies about immigrants focus on the past waves of immigration. Help students become more aware and sensitive to the struggles of new immigrants. Be sure to connect any study to your community by taking advantage of any local speakers, helping with a service project sponsored by a local organization, and so on. Launch a study by reading Eve Bunting's picture book for older readers *How Many Days to America? A Thanksgiving Story*, illustrated by Beth Peck (Clarion Books, 1990).

Music

Balgassi, Haemi. *Tae's Sonata*

Clément, Claude. *The Voice of the Wood*

Fenner, Carol. *Yolonda's Genius*

Handel, George Frideric. *Messiah: The Wordbook for the Oratorio.* Illus. by Barry Moser

Hurwitz, Johanna. *Leonard Bernstein: A Passion for Music*

Krull, Kathleen. *Lives of the Musicians: Good Times, Bad Times (And What the Neighbors Thought)*

MacLachlan, Patricia. *The Facts and Fictions of Minna Pratt*

Monceaux, Morgan. *Jazz: My Music, My People*

Namioka, Lensey. *Yang the Youngest and His Terrible Ear*

Nichol, Barbara. *Beethoven Lives Upstairs*

Raschka, Chris. *Charlie Parker Played Be Bop*

Weik, Mary Hays. *The Jazz Man*

Wolff, Virginia Euwer. *Mozart Season*

Asian American Fiction

American Dragons: Twenty-Five Asian American Voices. Edited by Laurence Yep

American Eyes: New Asian-American Short Stories for Young Adults. Edited by Lori M. Carlson

Balgassi, Haemi. *Tae's Sonata*

Chin, Fran. *Donald Duck*

Crew, Linda. *Children of the River*

Irwin, Hadley. *Kim/Kimi*

Jen, Gish. *Typical American*

Lee, Gus. *China Boy*

Lee, Marie G. *Finding My Voice*

Lee, Marie G. *If It Hadn't Been for Yoon Jun*

Lee, Marie G. *Necessary Roughness*

Lord, Bette Bao. *The Year of the Boar and Jackie Robinson*

Namioka, Lensey. *Yang the Second and Her Secret Admirers*

Yee, Paul. *Breakaway*

Yee, Paul. *Tales from Gold Mountain: Stories of the Chinese in the New World*

Cliques/Fitting In

Auch, Mary Jane. *Glass Slippers Give You Blisters*

Balgassi, Haemi. *Tae's Sonata*

Keller, Beverly. *Desdemona series*

Mills, Claudia. *Hannah on Her Way*

Naylor, Phyllis Reynolds. *Alice series*

Okimoto, Jean Davies. *Take a Chance, Gramps!*

Peters, Julie Anne. *Revenge of the Snob Squad*

Shreve, Susan. *The Gift of the Girl Who Couldn't Hear*

Shura, Mary Francis. *Polly Panic*

Vail, Rachel. *Wonder*

Wallace, Bill. *Beauty*

DeFelice, Cynthia

The Apprenticeship of Lucas Whitaker

LC 95-26728. 1996. 152p. $15.00 (ISBN 0-374-34669-0).
Farrar, Straus & Giroux. 1998. 160p. $4.50 pa.
(ISBN 0-380-72920-2 pa.). Camelot. 3 cassettes. 1997. $26.00
(ISBN 0-7887-0885-6). Recorded Books.

Genre: Historical fiction

Themes: Apprenticeships, tuberculosis, death, family life, grief, disease, superstitions, vampirism, scientific research, orphans, medicine, physicians, hope, kindness, microscopes

Reading level: Sixth grade

Interest level: Fifth through eighth grade

Reviews:
The Book Report. 15(5):32 March/April 1997.
Booklist. 93(3):348 October 1, 1996.
Bulletin of the Center for Children's Books.
    50(2):54 October 1996. (Recommended)
Horn Book. 73(1):55 January/February 1997.
School Library Journal. 42(8):142 August 1996.

Author Information

A professional storyteller and writer, Cynthia DeFelice previously was a school librarian. She makes appearances at libraries, workshops, festivals, and schools. DeFelice was raised with books; her mother was an English teacher. The books DeFelice liked best were the stories that made her feel as if she "was right in the story, part of what was happening." With her own writing, she attempts to "create an illusion of reality," but she sees her primary task as providing entertainment. "So I want to entertain, I want to keep my readers turning those pages! But I also want to leave them with a memory worth having, with characters they will remember and ideas they will come back to." Cynthia DeFelice lives in Geneva, New York, with her husband and two children.

Plot Summary

Twelve-year-old Lucas cannot save his family as one by one they succumb to tuberculosis. The year is 1849, and this highly contagious disease is sweeping the countryside. When Lucas learns of an unorthodox cure—exhuming the first family victim to tuberculosis and cutting out the heart—he is obsessed with guilt, thinking that he might have saved his loved ones. Kindly Doc Beecher takes Lucas on as an apprentice and teaches him to understand the difference between superstition and scientific fact.

Introducing the Book

The small typeface of this book may put off some readers, but the underlying vampire theme will intrigue most. Read aloud to the end of chapter 4 to capture interest. The medical afterword will be particularly interesting to teachers and parents.

Booktalks

On the Spot

One hundred fifty years ago, the hearts of some tuberculosis victims were cut out of their dead bodies and burned because people believed it would help cure others dying of the disease. Lucas Whitaker finds out the truth.

With the Author's Words

After all of Lucas's family dies of tuberculosis, he learns from Mr. Rood, his neighbor, that many believe the illness is caused by the undead.

"Undead?" Lucas repeated. "Yes," said Mr. Rood. "And, this being so, that person will then rise up from the grave and return to commit mischief on the living." "Wh-what kind of mischief?" Lucas

asked. Mr. Rood shifted uncomfortably. "They say he—or she—being desirous of sustenance, comes back to feed upon the living. To drain the very life from others in order to live himself." (pp. 8–9, hardback edition)

Fact or superstition? Was Lucas's family killed by the undead? Could he have saved them? His apprenticeship with a good doctor leads him to the answers.

Literature Extensions/Alternative Book Report Activities

Careers/Apprenticeships/Internship/Internet—Lucas is fortunate to become an apprentice to Doc Beecher, the local doctor, dentist, undertaker, barber, and pharmacist. Because of this experience, Lucas is well on his way to a career as a physician. It's not too early for middle school students to be thinking about future careers. Some programs like "Service Learning" and "School to Work" are essentially apprentice programs for students. Invite representatives to share information about these programs.

Helpful Internet sites include: "Welcome to Service-Learning" at http://csf.colorado.edu/sl/index.html and "School to Work" at http://www.stw.ed.gov/index.htm.

Also encourage participation in the April "Take Our Daughters to Work Day" program, which, in some areas, also includes participation by boys as well. "Take Our Daughters to Work Day" is held annually on the fourth Thursday in April. It is intended to give girls positive attention and to foster self-confidence during adolescence while giving them exposure to the work world. Information about the current year's program can be found by visiting the "Ms. Foundation" site at http://www.ms.foundation.org/.

Health/Epidemics/Tuberculosis/Internet—Tuberculosis (also known as consumption), an extremely contagious and deadly disease, killed all of Lucas's family and many of their friends. Vaccinations and antibiotics had nearly eradicated tuberculosis, but recently an antibiotic-resistant tuberculosis bacteria has developed and is becoming a health threat. Using standard research tools (periodical indexes, online databases, the Internet), students can discover the current status of this resistant bacteria. For more information about tuberculosis, consult *The Last Crusade: The War on Consumption, 1862–1954* by Mark Caldwell (Atheneum, 1988) and *Tuberculosis* by Alvin Silverstein (Enslow, 1994).

Other deadly epidemics, such as yellow fever, influenza, bubonic plague, small pox, and AIDS, have terrorized people since the beginning of time and continue to challenge scientists. Recently, the puzzle of the worldwide 1918 flu epidemic, when 20 million people perished, was solved. Researchers report that it was caused by a virus from American pigs and was closely related to swine flu. Provide the following books about epidemics for further reading and research: *When Plague Strikes: The Black Death, Smallpox and AIDS* by James Cross Giblin (HarperCollins, 1995); *Hygiene* by Don Nardo (Chelsea House, 1993); *Epidemic* by Christopher Lampton (Millbrook Press, 1992); and *The Hunt for Hidden Killers: Ten Cases of Medical Mystery* by Diane Yancey (Millbrook Press, 1994). One of many applicable Websites is "What About AIDS? Science, Art & Human Stories" at http://www.exploratorium.edu/AIDS/.

Health/Folk Medicine/Herbs/Internet—Doc Beecher sends Lucas to local herbalist Moll Garfield so he can learn about medicinal herbs. Herb lore and folk medicine continue to be of interest to many individuals.

Make the following reference books available for further information: *Rodale's Illustrated Encyclopedia of Herbs* by Claire Kowalchik and William H. Hylton (Rodale, 1987); *Earth Care Annual* (Rodale, 1990–); *Simon & Schuster's Guide to Plants and Flowers* by Francesco Bianchini and Azzurra Carrasa Pantano (Simon & Schuster, 1989); *Folk Medicine* by Marc Kusinitz (Chelsea House, 1991); *Encyclopedia of Herbs and Their Uses* by Deni Bown (Dorling Kindersley, 1995); *Medicinal Wild Plants* by Bradford Angier (Stackpole Books, 1995); and *Folk Remedies That Work* by Joan Wilen and Lydia Wilen (Harper-Perennial Library, 1996). Also visit the "Time Life Electronic Encyclopedia: Virtual Garden" at http://www.pathfinder.com/@@S3vZBQUAl811rCGh/vg/TimeLife/CG/vg-search.html for more information about herbs in North America.

Science/History of Medicine/Microscopes/Internet—Lucas's apprenticeship in the mid-1800s provided him with medical information and preliminary doctoring skills. Some students will be interested in the development of medicine throughout history. Provide them with: *Just What the Doctor Ordered: The History of American Medicine* by Brandon Marie Miller (Lerner Publications, 1997); *Colonial American Medicine* by

Susan Neiburg Terkel (Franklin Watts, 1993); *Health and Medicine* by David Ritchie, et al. (Chelsea House, 1995); and *The History of Health and Medicine* by Jenny Bryan (Raintree/Steck-Vaughn, 1996). Internet links from the "Scientific and Medical Antiques Pages" at http://www.utmem.edu/personal/thjones/sci_ant.htm will supplement a study and bring it into the twenty-first century.

Specific information about microscopes and their development may intrigue students as it did Lucas (see p. 145, hardback edition). Even if a microscope is unavailable to students, information can be located in *The Microscope Book* by Shar Johnstone and Leslie Johnstone (Sterling, 1997), or images viewed at the following Internet site: "Nanoworld Image Gallery" at http://www.uq.oz.au/nanoworld/images_1.html.

Novels of Superstition & Natural Healing

Cushman, Karen. *Catherine, Called Birdy*

Cushman, Karen. *The Midwife's Apprentice*

DeFelice, Cynthia. *The Apprenticeship of Lucas Whitaker*

De La Tour, Shatoiya. *The Herbalist of Yarrow: A Fairy Tale of Plant Wisdom*

Furlong, Monica. *Juniper*

Furlong, Monica. *Wise Child*

Lemieux, Anne. *Fruit Flies, Fish & Fortune Cookies*

Saller, Carol. *The Bridge Dancers*

Epidemics

DeFelice, Cynthia. *The Apprenticeship of Lucas Whitaker*

Farrell, Jeanette. *Invisible Enemies: Stories of Infectious Disease*

Fleischman, Paul. *Path of the Pale Horse*

Grifalconi, Ann. *Not Home*

Haddix, Margaret Peterson. *Running Out of Time*

Hudson, Jan. *Sweetgrass*

Johnston, Julie. *Hero of Lesser Causes*

Rockwood, Joyce. *To Spoil the Sun*

Towne, Mary. *Dive Through the Wave*

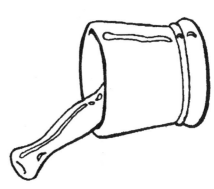

Practice, Practice, Practice—Apprentices

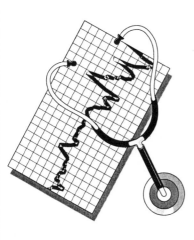

Alexander, Lloyd. *Westmark*

Cushman, Karen. *The Midwife's Apprentice*

DeFelice, Cynthia. *The Apprenticeship of Lucas Whitaker*

Fleischman, Paul. *Path of the Pale Horse*

Fleischman, Paul. *Saturnalia*

Krensky, Stephen. *The Printer's Apprentice*

Morrison, Taylor. *Antonio's Apprenticeship*

Morrison, Taylor. *The Neptune Fountain: The Apprenticeship of a Renaissance Sculptor*

Tomlinson, Theresa. *The Forestwife*

Fleischman, Sid
The 13th Floor: A Ghost Story

LC 94-42806. 1995. 134p. $15.00 (ISBN 0-688-14216-8). Greenwillow Books. 1997. 144p. $3.99 pa. (ISBN 0-440-41243-9 pa.). Yearling Books. *The 13th Floor: A Ghost Story* 2 cassettes read by Richard Adamson. 1995. $16.98 (ISBN 0-8072-7614-6). Listening Library.

Genres: Fantasy, adventure, humor

Themes: Time travel, brothers and sisters, ancestors, Puritans, witches, séances, orphans, pirates, superstitions, witch hunts, witch trials, lawyers, ghosts, trickery, orphans, buried treasure, battles

Reading level: Fourth grade

Interest level: Fourth through eighth grade

Reviews:
> *The Book Report.* 15(1):35 May/June 1996.
> *Booklist.* 92(3):314 October 1, 1995.
> *Bulletin of the Center for Children's Books.*
>   49(2):53 October 1995. (Recommended)
> *Horn Book.* 71(6):741 November/December 1995.
> *Publishers Weekly.* 242(41):86 October 9, 1995.
> *School Library Journal.* 95(10):133 October
>   1995.

Author Information

A self-trained magician via books from the public library, Sid Fleischman became an expert at sleight-of-hand tricks and later brought this talent to his writing. Born in New York in 1920, Fleischman grew up in San Diego and learned storytelling from his European father. He has been writing continually since the age of nineteen. Fleischman is father of Paul Fleischman, another popular award-winning children's author, and two daughters. Additional information about Fleischman can be found in his autobiography, *The Abracadabra Kid: A Writer's Life* (Greenwillow Books, 1996), and at this Internet site: http://www.bdd.com/bin/forums/teachers/flei.html.

He says he was inspired to write *The 13th Floor* when he found out that his wife was descended from a woman tried as a witch in early New England. "I knew I wanted to turn the event into a novel. The trouble was, I didn't think I'd be able to get any laughs out of the buckle-shoe Puritans I'd studied in school. I was wrong. The novel turned out to be one of my funniest."

Plot Summary

A cry for help from 300 years ago leads twelve-year-old Buddy and his grown-up sister back through time to save their ten-year-old ancestor Abigail from a Puritan witch trial. Buddy's wild adventures find him on a leaking pirate ship, surviving a howling storm at sea, accused of being a ghost, and cast adrift . . . and all before he even touches shore in Boston! The superstitions of the time fuel the witch hunt, but Abigail is saved through the clever tactics of Buddy and his sister, who just happens to be a fine lawyer. Their reward upon returning to the present is a unique treasure, courtesy of the pirates.

Introducing the Book

This light-hearted fantasy/adventure is fast-paced and funny. The 22 short chapters and author's note are accessible for most middle school readers. Tempt readers by using a booktalk or reading to the end of chapter 3.

Booktalks

On the Spot

When Buddy steps back in time from *The 13th Floor* to a pirate ship 300 years ago, the pirates think he's a ghost with his glow-in-the-dark shoe laces. But that's the least of his problems. Buddy needs to find his sister, save an ancestor on trial for being a witch, and find a way back through time.

(Consider making a permanent bookmark using glow-in-the-dark shoe laces and a printed copy of this booktalk.)

With the Author's Words

After listening to a strange message on his answering machine that directs him to "make haste" and come to the 13th floor, twelve-year-old Buddy rushes to a derelict building and painstakingly tries to make the elevator stop between the 12th and 14th floors.

I held my breath and opened the elevator door . . . I had found the thirteenth floor! I rushed forward into a windy, howling blackness. The elevator clanged shut after me and dropped away. A split second later I felt the floor heave up under me. I was pitched like a kicked cat into the wall at my left. Earthquake! I thought . . . . From the lights and shadows being flung about the room I saw now that it wasn't an earthquake that had struck me. I had found the thirteenth floor, and it was a ship at sea. (pp. 20–21, hardback edition)

Not only is the 13th floor a ship at sea, it's also 300 years back in time. Pirates, ghosts, witch trials—they are all there on *The 13th Floor*!

Literature Extensions/Alternative Book Report Activities

History/Pirates/Current Events/Internet—Students who enjoy the pirate adventures of *The 13th Floor* may want to investigate the facts about the "Golden Age of Piracy." In 1996, archaeologists recovered some artifacts, including a bell dated 1709, from what is believed to be the shipwreck of Blackbeard's *Queen Anne's Revenge*. Search the Internet subject directories and search engines for the current status and more information about that investigation.

An excellent Internet site about pirates is "National Geographic.com/kids: Pirates!" at http://www.nationalgeographic.com/features/97/pirates/maina.html, which features a pirate game, a Blackbeard page, and links to other pirate sites.

History/Witches/Mock Trials/Internet—Buddy ends up serving as Abigail's lawyer at a witchcraft trial. Students can learn more than Buddy knew about the law if they use the lesson plans and information about conducting mock trials in elementary, middle, and high schools that are available at such Internet sites as "Washington State Courts: Education" at http://www.wa.gov/courts/educate/home.htm.

Stage a mock trial and include a judge, a defense team, a prosecution team, witnesses, a selection of a fair jury, and an accused witch. Consider the suggestions below for other mock trials. Visit "Order in the Classroom" at "Taking the Courthouse to the Schoolroom" at http://www.rain.org/courthouse/order.htm for ideas about trials such as *101 Dalmatians vs. Cruella De Ville* and *The People vs. Darth 'E'-Vader*.

"The Wolf on Trial" in *School Library Journal* (39[9]:166 September 1993) has ideas about presenting Jon Scieszka's *The True Story of the 3 Little Pigs by A. Wolf* (Viking Kestrel, 1989). An easy adaptation of that trial would be the one featuring the "Big Bad Pig" from Eugene Triviza's *The Three Little Wolves and the Big Bad Pig* (Macmillan, 1993).

History/Salem Witch Trials/Internet—Many students may be shocked to discover that even ten-year-olds were on trial for witchcraft in 1692. Encourage students to visit the following Internet sites for interesting information: "The Salem Witch Trials 1692: A Chronology of Events" at http://www.salemweb.com/memorial/default.htm, "The Salem Witch Trials of 1692: A Brief Introduction" at http://www.salemweb.Com/witches.htm, "Accused of Witchcraft" at http://members.aol.com/samcasey/ancestors/witch.html, "Witch Hunt Hysteria" at http://www.adventure.com/library/encyclopedia/america/crucible.html, and "Joan's Witch Directory" at http://www.rci.rutgers.edu/~jup/witches.

Sociology/Superstitions/Folklore—Share *Anno's Medieval World* (Philomel Books, 1979) by Mitsumasa Anno as another example of a time when people believed pestilence was caused by demons and witches, and scientific thoughts (such as the world is round, not flat) could be considered heresy. Even after the Middle Ages, superstitions were passed on from generation to generation and were an integral part of the Puritan culture Buddy confronted when he traveled back in time to 1692. That year in Salem, twenty women were executed based on the fear, frenzy, and superstitions sparked by the visions of three young girls.

After students collect a list of the superstitions included in *The 13th Floor*, share other books on superstitions, such as: *Duck's Breath and Mouse Pie: A Collection of Animal Superstitions* by Steve Jenkins (Ticknor & Fields Books for Young Readers, 1994); *Don't Sing Before Breakfast, Don't Sleep in the Moonlight: Everyday Superstitions and How They Began* by Lila Perl (Houghton Mifflin, 1988); and *Cross Your Fingers, Spit in Your Hat: Superstitions and Other Beliefs* by Alvin Schwartz (HarperTrophy, 1993).

Ghost Stories

Bauer, Marion Dane. *A Taste of Smoke*

Bellairs, John. *The Ghost in the Mirror*

Cresswell, Helen. *Moondial*

Fleischman, Sid. *The 13th Floor: A Ghost Story*

Hahn, Mary Downing. *A Time for Andrew*

Hughes, Dean. *Nutty's Ghost*

Levin, Betty. *Marcy's Mill*

Lively, Penelope. *The Ghost of Thomas Kempe*

Service, Pamela F. *Phantom Victory*

Wiseman, David. *Jeremy Visick*

Wright, Betty Ren. *Haunted Summer*

Ship Ahoy: Pirate Stories

Avi. *Captain Grey*

Avi. *The True Confessions of Charlotte Doyle*

Fleischman, Sid. *The 13th Floor: A Ghost Story*

Gregory, Kristiana. *The Stowaway: A Tale of California Pirates*

Lasky, Kathryn. *Grace the Pirate*

Mahy, Margaret. *Tingleberries, Tuckertubs and Telephones: A Tale of Love and Ice-Cream*

McCully, Emily Arnold. *The Pirate Queen*

Scieszka, Jon. *The Not-So-Jolly Roger*

Stevenson, Robert Louis. *Treasure Island*

Yolen, Jane. *The Ballad of the Pirate Queens*

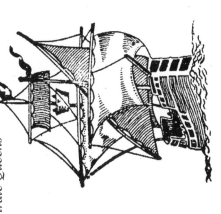

Time Slip . . . Back and Forth in Time

Barron, T. A. *Ancient One*

Fleischman, Sid. *The 13th Floor: A Ghost Story*

Conrad, Pam. *Stonewords: A Ghost Story*

Conrad, Pam. *Zoe Rising*

Cooney, Caroline B. *Both Sides of Time*

Cooney, Caroline B. *Out of Time*

Hahn, Mary Downing. *The Doll in the Garden: A Ghost Story*

Lunn, Janet. *The Root Cellar*

MacDonald, Reby Edmond. *The Ghosts of Austwick Manor*

Reiss, Kathryn. *Time Windows*

Slepian, Jan. *Back to Before*

Voigt, Cynthia. *Building Blocks*

Griffin, Peni R.
Margo's House

LC 95-51796. 1996. 122p. $16.00 (ISBN 0-689-80944-1).
Margaret K. McElderry/Simon & Schuster.

Genres: Fantasy, contemporary realistic fiction, adventure, multicultural

Themes: Fathers and daughters, love, dolls, dollhouses, African Americans, crafts, the paranormal, psychic phenomena, astral projections, souls, loyalty, unemployment, heart attacks, cats, woodworking, artisanship

Reading level: Fifth grade

Interest level: Fourth through eighth grade

Reviews:
The Book Report. 16(2):35 September/October 1997.
Booklist. 93(1):130 September 1, 1996.
Bulletin of the Center for Children's Books. 50(3):97 November 1996.
School Library Journal. 42(10):122 October 1996.

Author Information

Born in Texas, Peni R. Griffin depended on books as a child. Her family moved frequently, and books were her friends wherever she went. Her first stories were written at age five—in crayon—and Griffin says that now if she goes "more than three days without writing" she finds monsters under her bed. Griffin lives in San Antonio with her husband, Damon, who, she says, is the perfect writer's spouse. Learn more about Griffin by visiting her home page at http://www.geocities.com/athens/3401 or at http://www.txdirect.net/~griffin/0writing.htm. Send her e-mail at griffin@txdirect.net.

Plot Summary

Before Margo's unemployed father can finish the deluxe dollhouse and realistic dolls he is making for her, he has a serious heart attack. Terribly worried about him, Margo is drawn to the dollhouse for comfort. She continues the work on it and plays with the dolls, Butch and Sis. One night, Margo astrally projects into the body of Sis and becomes convinced that her father's survival depends on her.

Introducing the Book

Dolls that come "alive" have a special attraction to many readers, reluctant and otherwise. Read aloud the first two chapters (through p. 15, hardback edition) to grab attention.

Booktalks

On the Spot

Remember *The Indian in the Cupboard*? Who doesn't fantasize about small toys coming to life and having grand adventures? That's just what happens in *Margo's House*.

With the Author's Words

After Margo's dad is hospitalized with a heart attack, the special dollhouse he was building for her is mysteriously wallpapered one night. Margo struggles to find a reasonable explanation and ends up looking more carefully at the realistic dolls her dad had made.

> *Looked at one way, Margo could believe in toys having some kind of life. After all, they had heads and faces, hands and feet. When you played with them, you never had to decide how they would act. You just knew what their personalities were like, as if by telepathy. But how could a doll move even perfectly-jointed arms and legs, without muscles? How could painted wooden eyes see in the dark. . . . It didn't make sense. There must be some other explanation, but thinking wouldn't give it to her. She'd have to stay awake tonight, and see if anything happened. (p. 26, hardback edition)*

The goings-on are very strange in *Margo's House*. Stay awake with her to discover just how peculiar it becomes.

Literature Extensions/Alternative Book Report Activities

Arts and Crafts/Miniatures/Internet—Margo's dad is a careful and creative artist. The dollhouse and dolls he makes for her are constructed on a small scale with great attention to detail. Connect students to the concept of miniatures by pointing out that their action-figure toys are actually miniatures. Invite a miniaturist to talk about this craft and display handiwork. Many communities have organized groups who meet regularly to teach and work together. Contact the National Association of Miniature Enthusiasts (NAME) at http://www.miniatures.org or at P.O. Box 69, Carmel, IN 46032, phone number: (317) 571-8094, fax number: (317) 571-8105, for information about a group in your community.

Students can view other miniatures by looking at catalogs that may be borrowed from craft stores. Specific Internet Websites of interest include "The Delaware Toy & Miniature Museum" at http://www.thomes.net/toys/ and an electronic room-by-room tour of the Toy and Miniature Museum in Kansas City at http://www.umkc.edu/tmm/1floor.html.

Physics/Mechanics/Physiology—Butch is interested in the "mechanical problem" of the latch on the cat door (pp. 69–70, hardback edition), whereas Margo and her father are fascinated with the movements of the dolls. Provide books such as the following to assist students who ponder mechanical movements and physiology: *The Way Things Work* by David Macaulay (Houghton Mifflin, 1988); *Robots: Your High-Tech World* by Gloria Skurzynski (Bradbury Press, 1990); *How Dogs Really Work* by Alan Snow (Little, Brown and Company, 1995); *The Robot Zoo: A Mechanical Guide to the Way Animals Work* by John Kelly, Philip Whitfield, and Obin (Turner Publishing, 1994); and *The Body Atlas* by Mark Crocker (Oxford University Press, 1994).

Psychology/Psychic Phenomena—Reading more about psychic phenomena, the paranormal, astral projections, extrasensory perception, and other psychic events will be a high-interest project for many students. Assemble a classroom collection of books about these topics, including *How to Read Your Mother's Mind* by James M. Deem (Bantam Books, 1996); *How to Be a Fake Kreskin* by Kreskin (St. Martin's Press, 1996); *Psychic Sleuths: How Psychic Information Is Used to Help Solve Crimes* by Anita Larsen (New Discovery, 1994); *Psychic Connections: A Journey into the Mysterious World of PSI* by Lois Duncan and William George Roll (Delacorte Press, 1995); *Spooky Kids: Strange but True Tales* by Bruce M. Nash and Allan Zullo (Troll, 1994); and *Who Killed My Daughter?* by Lois Duncan (Delacorte Press, 1992).

Vocational Education/Woodcarving/Community Service—The construction of Margo's wooden dolls is described in detail and will pique the interest of many students. Share the pictures of the dolls in the following picture books: *Changes, Changes* by Pat Hutchins (Simon & Schuster, 1971); *The Tub People* (HarperCollins, 1989) and *The Tub Grandfather* (HarperCollins, 1993), both by Pam Conrad; and *The Wooden Doll* by Susan Bonners (Lothrop, Lee & Shepard, 1991). Using these books as inspiration, have students design wooden dolls using simple computer-assisted design (CAD) programs or manual graphing techniques. Select a production plan and then give the dolls to a charity holiday toy drive for distribution to needy children.

Psychic Phenomena

Cohen, Daniel. *Ghostly Warnings*

DeClements, Barthe, and Christopher Greims. *Double Trouble*

Duncan, Lois. *The Third Eye*

Griffin, Peni R. *Margo's House*

Kehert, Peg. *Danger at the Fair*

Mahy, Margaret. *The Haunting*

Matas, Carol, and Perry Nodelman. *More Minds*

Matas, Carol, and Perry Nodelman. *Of Two Minds*

Nash, Bruce M., and Allan Zullo. *Spooky Kids: Strange but True Tales*

Roberts, Willo Davis. *The Girl with the Silver Eyes*

Sargent, Sarah. *Watermusic*

Service, Pamela F. *Being of Two Minds*

Urton, Andrea. *Super Weird: Strange but True Stories You Won't Believe*

Little Folks

Banks, Lynne Reid. *Indian in the Cupboard* series

Clarke, Pauline. *Return of the Twelves*

Griffin, Peni R. *Margo's House*

Hodges, Margaret. *Gulliver in Lilliput*

Norton, Mary. *Borrowers* series

Peterson, John. *The Littles* series

Pratchett, Terry. *Truckers*

Swift, Jonathan. *Gulliver's Travels*

Winterfeld, Henry. *Castaways in Lilliput*

Winthrop, Elizabeth. *Castle in the Attic*

They're ALIVE!! Dolls

Banks, Lynne Reid. *Indian in the Cupboard* series

Bledsoe, Jerry. *The Angel Doll: A Christmas Story*

Cassedy, Sylvia. *Behind the Attic Wall*

Dexter, Catherine. *The Oracle*

Field, Rachel. *Hitty: Her First Hundred Years*

Griffin, Peni R. *Margo's House*

Kennedy, Richard. *Amy's Eyes*

MacDonald, Reby. *The Ghosts of Austwick Manor*

Nivola, Claire A. *Elisabeth*

Sleator, William. *Among the Dolls*

Turner, Ann. *Finding Walter*

Waugh, Sylvia. *The Mennyms* series

Winthrop, Elizabeth. *Castle in the Attic*

Wright, Betty Ren. *The Dollhouse Murders*

Gutman, Dan

The Million Dollar Shot

LC 97-6461. 1997. 114p. $13.95 (ISBN 0-7868-0334-7). Hyperion Books for Children.

Genres: Sports, contemporary realistic fiction, multicultural

Themes: Basketball, single-parent families, friendship, death, factories, contests, competition, poetry, money, rap, employment, pressure, coaching, opportunities, bribery, harassment, spying

Reading level: Fourth grade

Interest level: Fourth through eighth grade

Reviews:
> *Booklist.* 94(3):329 October 1, 1997.
> *School Library Journal.* 43(12):124 December 1997.

Author Information

Born in New York and raised in New Jersey, Dan Gutman was two years into a psychology master's program at Rutgers University when he realized he preferred writing to psychoanalyzing. Like many middle grade boys, Gutman disliked reading until he found books written about his favorite subject—baseball. Then he read everything he could find. Interested in providing stories for reluctant readers, particularly boys, Gutman writes about sports even though he claims he was and is a "terrible athlete."

Plot Summary

Sixth-grader Eddie Ball wins a poetry contest, allowing him the opportunity to make a free throw at the NBA finals for $1 million. His friend Annie and her father (a former basketball star) help him train. A series of pranks and an attempt at outright bribery nearly ruin Eddie's chances, but he keeps his calm and rises to the occasion.

Introducing the Book

This easier-to-read book will appeal to a wide audience. The story, featuring both a boy and a girl, is fast-paced, funny, and exciting. Read aloud chapter 1, continuing to the end of the first sentence of chapter 2.

Booktalks

On the Spot

How would you like to earn $1 million for one second of work? It's one shot in a million.

With the Author's Words

Eddie enters a poetry contest sponsored by Finkle Foods in which the winner gets a chance at shooting a free throw and winning $1 million.

> *You know, I could keep you in suspense for a long time. I could tell you about the three million entries Finkle Foods received from kids all over the country. I could tell you about all the articles on the contest that appeared in newspapers and magazines. I could make you read a bunch of pages in this book before I reveal what happened in the contest. I could do that, but I won't. That would be cruel. Besides, I'm busting inside. I have to tell you right away. (p. 34, hardback edition)*

I have to tell you, too. The answer is . . . *The Million Dollar Shot.*

Literature Extensions/Alternative Book Report Activities

Contests/Cooking/Internet—Most kids, like Eddie and Annie, love to enter contests. Provide a variety of entry blanks for current contests and encourage students to enter one or more of their choice. Many children's magazines include contest information. Some of these competitions test skills in cooking, writing, athletics, art, video production, and so forth.

For more contest ideas, consult *All the Best Contests for Kids* by Joan M. Bergstrom and Craig Bergstrom (5th edition, Ten Speed Press, 1995) and *The Ultimate Guide to Student Contests: Grades 7–12* by Scott Pendleton (Walker, 1997).

Search the Internet for contests sponsored by organizations such as "Crayola Kids" and "Thinkquest."

Language Arts/Poetry/Rap—Eddie makes an earnest but pathetic attempt at writing a rap poem for the poetry contest. Rap is an appealing poetry and music form for many students. Encourage them to write about their own lives and worlds in rap and provide some of the following books as examples: *Nathaniel Talking* (Black Butterfly Children's Books, 1988) and *Night on Neighborhood Street* (Dial, 1991), both by Eloise Greenfield; *Chicka Chicka Boom Boom* by Bill Martin Jr. and John Archambault (Simon & Schuster, 1989); *Yo, Hungry Wolf! A Nursery Rap* by David Vozar (Delacorte Press, 1993); and the rap poems that begin each chapter of *The Mouse Rap* by Walter Dean Myers (Harper & Row, 1990).

Math/Concepts—Like most people, Eddie wonders "how much is a million dollars?" In order for your students to understand this concept, provide *Max Makes a Million* by Maira Kalman (Viking, 1990) and *How Much Is a Million?* by David Schwartz (William Morrow & Company, 1987).

Other mathematical picture books include *Counting on Frank* by Rod Clement (Gareth Stevens Publishing, 1991); *Math Curse* by Jon Scieszka (Viking, 1995); and *The Librarian Who Measured the Earth* by Kathryn Lasky (Little, Brown and Company, 1994). Picture books about other mathematical concepts, such as factorials, include *A Grain of Rice* by Helena Clare Pittman (Hastings House, 1986); *Anno's Multiplying Jar* by Mitsumasa Anno (Philomel Books, 1983); and *The Rajah's Rice: A Mathematical Folktale from India,* adapted by David Barry (W. H. Freeman & Co., 1994).

Sports/History—Eddie is coached to shoot free throws by Annie's dad, who is a talented basketball player. Use this book as an impetus to point student research to other great shooters in a variety of sports. To get them started, suggest individuals like Annie Oakley, Tiger Woods, Wayne Gretsky, Michael Jordan, Robin Hood, Pelé, and so on. Have a group brainstorming session to come up with others and determine the focus of the research.

Just One Parent

Byars, Betsy. *McMummy*

Conly, Jane Leslie. *Crazy Lady!*

Duder, Tessa. *Jellybean*

Farrell, Mame. *Bradley and the Billboard*

Fine, Anne. *Alias Madame Doubtfire*

Fine, Anne. *Step by Wicked Step*

Griffin, Adele. *Split Just Right*

Gutman, Dan. *The Million Dollar Shot*

Hest, Amy. *Pete and Lily*

Hurwitz, Johanna. *DeDe Takes Charge!*

Mead, Alice. *Junebug*

Paulsen, Gary. *Hatchet*

Hoops

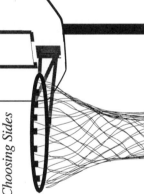

Burleigh, Robert. *Hoops*

Christopher, Matt. *Red-hot Hightops*

Cooper, Ilene. *Choosing Sides*

Draper, Sharon M. *Blowing Bubbles with the Enemy*

Glenn, Mel. *Jump Ball: A Basketball Season in Poems*

Greenfield, Eloise. *For the Love of the Game: Michael Jordan and Me*

Gutman, Dan. *The Million Dollar Shot*

Hughes, Dean. *Go to the Hoop!*

Hurwitz, Johanna. *Even Stephen*

Pfeffer, Susan Beth. *Sara Kate, Superkid*

Quattlebaum, Mary. *Jackson Jones and the Puddle of Thorns*

And the Winner Is . . .

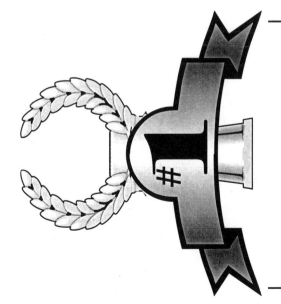

Bunting, Eve. *Nasty, Stinky Sneakers*

Gutman, Dan. *The Million Dollar Shot*

Kline, Suzy. *Orp and the Chop Suey Burgers*

Manes, Stephen. *Make Four Million Dollars by Next Thursday*

Naylor, Phyllis Reynolds. *Beetles, Lightly Toasted*

Peters, Julie Anne. *The Stinky Sneakers Contest*

Hobbs, Will
Kokopelli's Flute

LC 95-8422. 1995. 148p. $15.00 (ISBN 0-689-31974-6). Atheneum.
1997. 165p. $4.50pa. (ISBN 0-380-72818-4pa.). Camelot.
3 cassettes/4 hours. $26.00 (ISBN 0-7887-0599-7). Recorded Books.

Genres: Fantasy, adventure, mystery, contemporary realistic fiction, multicultural

Themes: Indians of North America, ruins, magic, archaeology, paleontology, ecology, farming, transformations, Anasazi, flutes, cliff dwellings, antiquities, hantavirus, symbols, survival, grave robbing, seeds, desert animals, rock art, vandalism, theft, drought, dogs, artifacts, deforestation

Reading level: Fifth grade

Interest level: Fourth through ninth grade

Reviews:
> *Booklist.* 92(3):304 October 1, 1995.
> *Kliatt Paperback and Audio Book Guide.* 31(4):16 July 1997.
> *School Library Journal.* 41(10):134 October 1995. (Starred review)
> *Voice of Youth Advocates.* 18(6):372 February 1996. (#4 quality, #4 popularity)

Author Information

A former English and reading teacher in Colorado, Will Hobbs is a graduate of Stanford University. His home in Durango, Colorado, is near the Weminuche Wilderness, and he frequently goes backpacking with his family and friends. Often, Hobbs travels to remote areas to visit ruins like those in *Kokopelli's Flute*. For a long time, Hobbs has been interested in the ancient peoples of the Southwest and their amazing homes carved into the cliffs. He has an abiding affection for "wild places and the other creatures with whom we share the planet" and hopes that he can elicit those same feelings in his readers. An interview with Hobbs is available on the Internet at http://www.amazon.com/.

Plot Summary

Thirteen-year-old Tepary is hiding when he sees two men robbing an ancient grave in an Anasazi cliff dwelling. After they leave, he can't resist blowing into the (Kokopelli magic) bone flute they have dropped. From that time on, Tep is transformed nightly into a packrat. In addition to trying to undo the transformations, Tep's other challenges include catching the robbers, helping his father with their experimental farming and seed business when he is in his boy body, and not eating the seeds and plants when he is in his packrat body. Help comes in the form of a mysterious old man from the past, who also saves Tep's mother from a deadly virus while teaching him about the past and the future.

Introducing the Book

To capture potential readers, read aloud to the bottom of page 19 (hardback edition) where Tep experiences his first transformation. The large font size and continual action are great selling points. Consider introducing *Kokopelli's Flute* by reading aloud *Dreamplace* by George Ella Lyon (Orchard, 1993), a picture book that blends the past and the present in the American Southwest.

Booktalks

On the Spot

The magic of ancient things draws Tep into a cycle of transformation. In the day, he's a boy scrambling through ancient cliff dwellings; in the night . . . he's a packrat.

With the Author's Words

After Tep blows on the ancient Indian flute, strange things began to happen . . . .

> *I remember putting the flute to my lips and blowing on it a minute or two. The notes I was producing sounded as pure as falling water. I remember starting to feel dizzy . . . the room started spinning and reeling. . . . Next thing I knew, I had the sensation of having long black whiskers radiating out*

from my face . . . I didn't feel anything like myself, and when I looked at my hands, I could see why. I was looking at the five-clawed fingers of . . . a rat. I felt the bottom of my spine moving, and out of the corner of my eye I could see a tail, a long, bushy tail. (pp. 18–19, hardback edition)

Tep's transformations become a nightly occurrence, and his rat-self is very difficult to control. It's all part of Kokopelli's magic . . . and mystery.

Literature Extensions/Alternative Book Report Activities

Archaeology/Cliff Dwellings/Anasazi/Internet—Cliff dwellings and Native American ruins, like those featured in *Kokopelli's Flute*, are scattered throughout the American Southwest. Careful excavation of these sites gives information about the fascinating Anasazi culture and society through the discoveries of artifacts, seeds, art, and the like. Exploration of the following Internet sites can enhance understanding of these people and their times: "Anasazi Indian Village" at http://www.infowest.com/anasazi/index.html, "Anasazi" at http://www.so-utah.com/feature/anasazi/homepage.html, and "Anasazi Archaeology" at http://www.swcolo.org/Tourism/ArchaeologyHome.html.

Book connections include *Dreamplace* by George Ella Lyon (Orchard, 1993); *The Ancient Cliff Dwellers of Mesa Verde* by Caroline Arnold (Clarion Books, 1992); *In Search of the Old Ones: Exploring the Anasazi World of the Southwest* by David Roberts (Simon & Schuster, 1996); *Anasazi* by Leonard Everett Fisher (Atheneum, 1997); *The Anasazi* by Eleanor H. Ayer (Walker & Company, 1993); *Ancient Indians: The First Americans* by Roy Gallant (Enslow Publishers, 1989); and *Cities in the Sand: The Ancient Civilizations of the Southwest* by Scott Warren (Chronicle Books, 1992).

Art/Rock Art/Archaeology/Indians of North America/Internet—Tep is able to solve the mystery of his transformation by studying the ancient drawings on the wall of Picture House, an Anasazi cave. Ancient pictographs and petroglyphs reveal information about Native American history, culture, and legend. For further study, provide students with some of the following books: *Native American Rock Art: Messages from the Past* by Yvette La Pierre (Lickle Publishing, 1994); *Prehistoric Rock Art* by Marinella Terzi (Childrens Press, 1993); *Stories in Stone: Rock Art Pictures by Early Americans* by Caroline Arnold (Clarion Books, 1996); and *Rock Art: Images from the Ancient Ones* by Jennifer Owings Dewey (Little, Brown and Company, 1996).

Visit these two "Rock Art" Internet sites: http://net.indra.com/~doak/rockart.html and http://www-personal.umich.edu/~bclee/rockart/rockart.html, which has numerous other links.

Health/Hantavirus/Centers for Disease Control/Internet—The characters in *Kokopelli's Flute* are constantly aware of the danger of contracting hantavirus, a potentially fatal disease believed to be contracted by breathing dust from rodent droppings. Students can learn how this disease was discovered, current information on the disease, and the status of research by exploring the specific hantavirus Web page at "The Centers for Disease Control" at http://www.cdc.gov/ncidod/diseases/hanta/hps/index.htm.

History/Time Capsules/Internet—Tep's mother learns much about the past by studying old nests. In particular, she examines *middens* ("rat-dung heaps"), which provide a record of antiquity by virtue of the seeds and other treasures collected by packrats in these natural "time capsules." The idea of time capsules is fascinating, and students will enjoy creating their own. What items will students select to reflect their time and individual personalities? The International Time Capsule Society recommends the following steps: 1) Select an opening date, such as high school graduation day; 2) choose a container with a cool, dry, and dark interior; 3) locate a secure location, such as a building cornerstone or storage area, and mark that spot with a description of the time capsule's mission; 4) gather items with a mix of materials and an inventory; and 5) have a formal sealing ceremony and photograph the time capsule's contents.

Visit "Time Capsules: Archival Protection" at http://www.si.edu/cal/timecaps.html for further instructions.

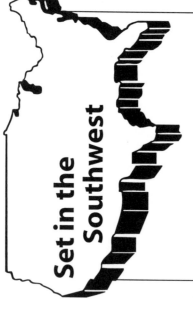

Set in the Southwest

Baylor, Byrd. *The Desert Is Theirs*

Baylor, Byrd. *Desert Voices*

Cannon, A. E. *The Shadow Brothers*

Hobbs, Will. *Beardance*

Hobbs, Will. *Beardream*

Hobbs, Will. *Bearstone*

Hobbs, Will. *Kokopelli's Flute*

Mikaelson, Ben. *Sparrow Hawk Red*

Myers, Walter Dean. *The Righteous Revenge of Artemis Bonner*

Rostkowski, Margaret. *Moon Dancer*

Skurzynski, Gloria. *Trapped in Sliprock Canyon*

Another Body: Tales of Transformation

Berenzy, Alix. *A Frog Prince*

Cooper, Susan. *The Selkie Girl*

Hobbs, Will. *Kokopelli's Flute*

Jones, Diana Wynne. *The Ogre Downstairs*

Luenn, Nancy. *Arctic Unicorn*

Martin, Rafe. *The Boy Who Lived with the Seals*

McDermott, Gerald. *Raven*

McKinley, Robin. *Beauty: A Retelling of the Story of Beauty and the Beast*

McKinley, Robin. *Rose Daughter*

Murphy, Claire Rudolf. *The Prince and the Salmon People*

Pierce, Meredith Ann. *The Woman Who Loved Reindeer*

Magic Indian Powers from the Past

Barron, T. A. *The Ancient One*

Hobbs, Will. *Kokopelli's Flute*

Katz, Welwyn Wilton. *False Face*

Paulsen, Gary. *Canyons*

Paulsen, Gary. *The Legend of the Red Horse Cavern*

Lasky, Kathryn. *A Voice in the Wind*

Steiner, Barbara. *Ghost Cave*

Jackson, Donna

The Bone Detectives: How Forensic Anthropologists Solve Crimes and Uncover Mysteries of the Dead

LC 95-19051. 1996. 48p. $16.95 (ISBN 0-316-82935-8). Little, Brown and Company.

Genres: Nonfiction, mystery

Themes: Forensic anthropology, science, bones, forensics, anthropology, crimes, death, investigations, fingerprints, DNA, fossils, detectives, police, photography, sculpting, skulls, skeletons, murders, clues

Reading level: Seventh grade

Interest level: Fifth through twelfth grade

Reviews:
Booklist. 92(15):1358 April 1, 1996.
Bulletin of the Center for Children's Books. 49(8):267 April 1996. (Recommended)
Horn Book. 72(3):348–49 May/June 1996.
School Library Journal. 42(5):123 May 1996. (Starred review)
Voice of Youth Advocates. 19(3):178–79 August 1996. (#5 quality, #3 popularity)

Author Information

Donna Jackson is an award-winning author and has published articles and stories in magazines and newspapers. She developed a fascination for forensics after she interviewed a bone detective, Dr. Michael Charney, for a newspaper story. Jackson has a journalism degree from the University of Colorado in Boulder and writes a monthly children's column for the *Greeley Tribune*. She lives in Louisville, Colorado, with her husband and son.

Plot Summary

In order to explain the techniques and the science of forensic anthropology, Jackson reconstructs an investigation centered on the discovery of a human skeleton buried at a remote Missouri Boy Scout camp. Additional information is presented in the book's acknowledgment, glossary, and a "bone biography."

Introducing the Book

The combination of murder-mystery and forensic investigation make this a high-interest book for most readers, despite the long sentences and scientific terminology. The layout is appealing with plenty of white space, single- and double-page spreads, intriguing headlines, and a multitude of color photographs. To introduce the book, read aloud the quotation by Dr. Snow facing the table of contents page: "As those who study them have come to learn, bones make good witnesses—although they speak softly, they never lie and they never forget."

Students can view a video version of this investigation, including some of the same photographs, on the Discovery Channel's series called *The New Detectives: Case Studies in Forensic Science*.

Booktalks

On the Spot

Read *The Bone Detectives* to discover the stories bones can tell about their life . . . and their death.

With the Author's Words

More than two hundred bones hold our bodies together, and each one tells a story. Some reveal our height. Some divulge our race and sex. Some even share information about foods we've eaten, limbs we've broken, and diseases we've suffered. Not every bone tattles freely, however. Some bones say more than others. But they all tell their secrets to the few who speak their language: forensic anthropologists. . . . (p. 7)

. . . also known as *The Bone Detectives*!

Literature Extensions/Alternative Book Report Activities

Careers/Police and Detectives/Internet—Investigations of crimes today include the use of age-old techniques in combination with modern technology. Visit a police lab to learn more about this work and to find out about DNA, fingerprints, and other crime-solving methods. Introduce students to books on crime solving, such as *Crime Lab 101: Experimenting with Crime Detection* by Robert Gardner (Silver Moon Press, 1994).

The Forensic Science section of the "Kid's and Youth Education Page" at the FBI at http://www.fbi.gov/kids/forensic/forensic.htm includes information about DNA analysis, polygraph tests, and fingerprint identification.

Careers/Science—Some students may find forensic anthropology intriguing as a career choice. Invite a forensic anthropologist to answer questions about what they do. Create a classroom library of books detailing forensic investigations. Include *Crime Science* by Vivien Bowers (Owl/Firefly, 1997); *Threads of Evidence: Using Forensic Science to Solve Crimes* by Herma Silverstein (Twenty-First Century, 1996); *Crime Lab 101* by Robert Gardner (Walker & Company, 1992); and *Crime Fighting* by Ian Graham (Raintree/Steck-Vaughn, 1995). Also collect books listed on the bookmark "Science Detectives: The Bones Know" for specific information regarding excavations.

Games/Cooperative Learning—Students can solve their own mysteries using forensic clues. Modify one of the many murder-mystery games available for group participation. Stage a crime scene with bones and clues and divide students into teams. For a true cross-curricular experience, the crime-solving teams should include a photographer, a forensic anthropologist, a detective, a journalist, and so forth.

Books with activity ideas include *The Investigation of Murder (Crimebusters)* by Brian Lane (Copper Beech Books, 1996) and *Detective Science: 40 Crime-Solving, Case-Breaking, Crook-Catching Activities for Kids* by Jim Wiese (John Wiley & Sons, 1996).

Science/Biology/Skeletons—Introduce a traditional study of skeletons by reading aloud *Dem Bones* by Bob Barner (Chronicle Books, 1996). Expand this study to include forensics. Forensic anthropologist Dr. Charney describes which bones in particular divulge specific information. For instance, information gained by inspecting a skull can often identify ethnic origin and gender; pubic bones offer clues concerning gender and number of births; and limb bones can indicate height. Using a skeletal diagram such as the "Bone Biography" included in *The Bone Detectives* or the one in *The Visual Dictionary of Human Anatomy* (Dorling Kindersley, 1996), students can expand traditional bone labeling to include explanations of which bones give information about gender, height, weight, racial differences, age markers, and the like.

Science Detectives: The Bones Know

Buried in Ice: The Mystery of a Lost Arctic Expedition by Owen Beattie and John Geiger

The Case of the Mummified Pigs by Susan E. Quinlan

Crime Science by Vivien Bowers

Dead Men Do Tell Tales: The Strange & Fascinating Cases of a Forensic Anthropologist by William R. Maples

Discovering the Iceman: What Was It Like to Find a 5,300-Year-Old Mummy? by Shelley Tanaka

Fingerprints and Talking Bones by Charlotte Foltz Jones

The Fire Curse and Other True Medical Mysteries by David Lee Drotar

Frozen Man by David Getz

The Iceman by Don Lessem

Mummies and Their Mysteries by Charlotte Wilcox

Talking Bones: The Science of Forensic Anthropology by Peggy Thomas

Kids Solving Crimes: You Can Do It

The Bone Detectives: How Forensic Anthropologists Solve Crimes and Uncover Mysteries of the Dead by Donna Jackson

Crime Lab 101: Experimenting with Crime Detection by Robert Gardner

Detective Dictionary: A Handbook for Aspiring Sleuths by Erich Ballinger

Detective Science: 40 Crime-Solving, Case-Breaking, Crook-Catching Activities for Kids by Jim Wiese

The Ghostwriter Detective Guide: Tools and Tricks of the Trade by Susan Lurie

The Ghostwriter Detective Guide 2: More Tools and Tricks of the Trade by Jordan Brown et al.

The Investigation of Murder (Crimebusters) by Brian Lane

The Young Detective's Handbook by William Vivian Butler

Kid Sleuths: Mystery Stories

Byars, Betsy. *Herculeah Jones* mysteries

Coville, Bruce. *The A. I. Gang: Operation Sherlock*

George, Jean Craighead. *The Fire Boy Connection*

Hahn, Mary Downing. *Dead Man in Indian Creek*

Hayes, Daniel. *The Trouble with Lemons*

Howe, James. *Sebastian Barth* mysteries

Kehret, Peg. *Danger at the Fair*

Roberts, Willo Davis. *Scared Stiff*

Jukes, Mavis

Expecting the Unexpected: Sex Ed with Mrs. Gladys B. Furley, R.N.

LC 96-2464. 1996. 132p. $15.95 (ISBN 0-385-32242-9). Delacorte Press

Genres: Contemporary realistic fiction, humor

Themes: Girls, sisters, mothers and daughters, school life, family life, teachers, physical development, sex education, pranks, menstruation, pregnancy, friendship, adolescents, misunderstanding, responsibility, menopause, middle age, art, drawing, graphic artists, contests, crushes

Reading level: Fourth grade

Interest level: Fourth through eighth grade

Reviews:
> *The Book Report.* 15(2):39 September/October 1996.
> *Booklist.* 93(3):342 October 1, 1996.
> *Bulletin of the Center for Children's Books.* 50(4):140 December 1996.
> *Publishers Weekly.* 243(35):98 August 26, 1996.
> *School Library Journal.* 42(9):202 September 1996.

Author Information

Mavis Jukes grew up in the East, went to college in Colorado and California, taught school, became a lawyer, and eventually began writing children's books after the birth of her first daughter. As a child, she loved nature and spent much time chasing fireflies and having rotten tomato fights with her brother and sister. As an adult, her interests remain much the same. Jukes now lives in Sonoma County, California, with her husband and two teenage daughters.

Plot Summary

Twelve-year-old River doesn't want to hear all the sex ed information Mrs. Furley is sharing with the sixth-grade class. She'd rather skip menstrual cramps and go straight to menopause. However, River does pick up enough information to suspect that her teenage sister is pregnant. In addition to this suspicion, River's days are filled with sketching a design for the school breezeway; plotting and executing pranks against their nice teacher, Mr. Elmo; and trying to win the "Class with Class" award. Misunderstandings, tricks, and unforeseen events keep River guessing.

Introducing the Book

The personal nature of the story, the frank dialogue, and the lower reading level of this title points to on-your-own reading. The humor and subject matter will delight middle grade students, especially girls, and the title alone will make this book popular.

Any school offering a comprehensive sexuality curriculum should have this book available. The information is age-appropriate and accurate. Jukes's well-received informational book on human growth and development, *It's a Girl Thing: How to Stay Healthy, Safe, and in Charge* (Alfred A. Knopf, 1997), is a terrific companion title.

Booktalks

On the Spot

River would prefer that facts about sex ed remain a mystery. But Mrs. Furley thinks growing up is as exciting as going to a party, and she expects River to attend. The "party" *is* exciting . . . and hilarious . . . and, in spite of herself, River just might discover exactly what she needs to know.

With the Author's Words

Students in Mr. Elmo's sixth-grade class can't resist playing pranks on him, and River knows that hiding an unmentionable object in his hat is sure to be hilarious.

> *Given the number of students who now knew about the hat trick, and given that every student signed a pledge not to fool around about stuff related to Human Interaction class, and given the fact that every last student who knew about the trick continued to dishonor this pledge by sitting in Sustained Silent Reading daydreaming about the moment when Mr. Elmo would discover the latest alteration to his clothing, River had a question: Should the class still even be considered for the Class With Class contest? You had to wonder. (p. 85, hardback edition)*

Expect the unexpected when you read this funny book.

Literature Extensions/Alternative Book Report Activities

Art/Collage—The cover of this book is a collage, consisting of illustrations that highlight events in the story. Using this as an example, students can create a collage depicting a time period in middle or junior high school. The titles of their pieces can be reflective of the events portrayed.

Health/Human Development/Sexuality Education—River's sixth-grade class is taking a comprehensive sexuality education course taught by a qualified nurse. Course content includes male and female development, sexually transmitted diseases, information about Planned Parenthood, and so on. Develop a classroom library focused on sex education. Include *Expecting the Unexpected* plus the following titles: *It's a Girl Thing: How to Stay Healthy, Safe, and in Charge* by Mavis Jukes (Alfred A. Knopf, 1996); *The Period Book: Everything You Don't Want to Ask—But Need to Know* by Karen Gravelle (Walker & Company, 1996); and *It's Perfectly Normal: Changing Bodies, Growing Up, Sex, and Sexual Health* by Robie H. Harris (Candlewick Press, 1996), as well as *What's Happening to Me? The Answer to Some of the World's Most Embarrassing Questions* (L. Stuart, 1975) and *Where Did I Come From? The Facts of Life Without Any Nonsense and with Illustrations* (L. Stuart, 1973), both by Peter Mayle.

Health/Human Development/History—Part of what River and her classmates learn about in their Human Interaction class concerns premenstrual syndrome (PMS). Students can learn more about this historically misunderstood syndrome by doing further research. Helpful books include *Everything You Need to Know About PMS (Premenstrual Syndrome)* by Barbara A. Moe (Rosen Publisher Group, 1995); *Once a Month: The Original Premenstrual Syndrome Handbook* by Katharina Dalton (Hunter House, 1994); and *PMS: Premenstrual Syndrome: A Guide for Young Women* by Gilda Berger (Hunter House, 1991).

Reading/Schoolwide Activities—Two interesting school activities are detailed in this book. The upper-grade classes compete in a "Class with Class" award program. Replicate this in your school. The scoring system and great prizes are found on pages 13–14 in the hardback edition.

River mentions participation in Sustained Silent Reading (SSR). Research has shown that students who read daily in SSR programs and who see adults modeling the same activity become significantly better readers. Furthermore, the benefits are greatest if SSR is done schoolwide rather than randomly in individual classrooms. There are even some schools where the principal, secretaries, custodians, and visitors read!

SSR is a simple, cost-free program that can easily be implemented in any school or classroom. The following are the basic guidelines: 1) Set aside an appropriate amount of reading time (usually fifteen minutes) daily; 2) every student selects reading material—books, newspapers, comics, magazines, and the like, that will be read for the entire time; 3) Everyone reads. There will be no filing fingernails or grading papers; and 4) reports are not required. Records are not kept.

Laughing Out Loud

Byars, Betsy. *Bingo Brown, Gypsy Lover*

Byars, Betsy. *Bingo Brown's Guide to Romance*

Gantos, Jack. *Head or Tails: Stories from the Sixth Grade*

Jukes, Mavis. *Expecting the Unexpected: Sex Ed with Mrs. Gladys B. Furley, R.N.*

Paulsen, Gary. *Harris and Me: A Summer Remembered*

Spinelli, Jerry. *Crash*

Spinelli, Jerry. *Space Station Seventh Grade*

Spinelli, Jerry. *Who Put That Hair in My Toothbrush?*

FACTS: What's Hap-pening to My Body?

Gravelle, Karen. *The Period Book: Everything You Don't Want to Ask (But Need to Know)*

Harris, Robie H. *It's Perfectly Normal: Changing Bodies, Growing Up, Sex, and Sexual Health*

Isler, Charlotte, and Alwyn T. Cohall. *The Watts Teen Health Dictionary*

Jukes, Mavis. *It's a Girl Thing: How to Stay Healthy, Safe, and in Charge*

Mayle, Peter. *What's Happening to Me? The Answer to Some of the World's Most Embarrassing Questions*

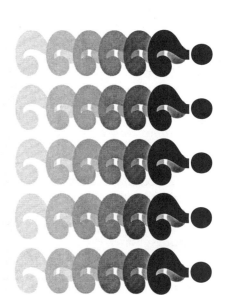

Girls, Girls, Girls

Blume, Judy. *Are You There, God? It's Me, Margaret*

Delton, Judy. *Angel series*

Jukes, Mavis. *Expecting the Unexpected: Sex Ed with Mrs. Gladys B. Furley, R.N.*

Keller, Beverly. *Desdemona series*

Lowry, Lois. *Anastasia series*

Naylor, Phyllis Reynolds. *Alice series*

Rocklin, Joanne. *For Your Eyes Only!*

Shreve, Susan Richards. *The Bad Dreams of a Good Girl*

 Krull, Kathleen

Lives of the Athletes: Thrills, Spills (And What the Neighbors Thought)

illustrated by
Kathryne Hewitt

LC 95-50702. 1997. 96p. $19.00 (ISBN 0-15-200806-3). Harcourt Brace & Company.

Genres: Biography, nonfiction, sports, multicultural

Themes: Athletes, sports, Olympics, heroes, self-esteem, courage, racism, gender equity, role models, movies, public relations, charity, track and field, baseball, swimming, tennis, basketball, football, surfing, golf, volleyball, soccer, ice hockey, figure skating, mountain climbing, martial arts

Reading level: Eighth grade

Interest level: Fourth through ninth grade

Reviews:
  Booklist. 93(14):1241 March 15, 1997.
  Bulletin of the Center for Children's Books. 50(10):363 June 1997. (Recommended)
  School Library Journal. 43(5):146–47 May 1997.

Author Information

When Kathleen Krull was fifteen, she was fired from her part-time library job because she was reading when she was supposed to be working. Her love for reading didn't go away, and immediately after college graduation Krull began working in the children's book publishing field. Some of her writing projects include some of the Trixie Belden series, a collection of Christmas carols, and a series of twenty-four concept books. Krull says: "I love getting the chance to explore subjects I'm passionate about . . . and making them meaningful for kids. I'm nosy about people, for example, and the Lives of . . . series allows me to snoop behind the closed doors of some of my favorite groups of (really strange) people. This series, by the way, is not so different from a book I made when I was ten—it was called *Hair-Do's and People I Know* and starred strange girls, boys, nuns, trees, and lots of hair." Find out more about Krull at "Author at a Glance" at http://www.friend.ly.net/scoop/biographies/kkrull.html by Harcourt Brace & Company.

Plot Summary

These unusual, illustrated biographical sketches feature twenty of the best athletes of the twentieth century. Discover their moments of glory (African American Jesse Owens won four Olympic gold medals in Germany when Hitler was proclaiming whites the supreme race), their quirks (Babe Ruth snacked on pickled eels with chocolate ice cream), and more. The book includes a bibliography.

Introducing the Book

Despite the high reading level, students will use this book (and the others in the series) for both recreational reading and to satisfy biography assignments. The combination of realistic and cartoon illustrations, the unusual and attractive layout, and the large areas of white space are visually appealing. Entice readers by sharing aloud selected biographical sketches.

Booktalks

On the Spot

Did you know that surfing was a sport for Hawaiian kings? And that Babe Ruth snacked on pickled eels with chocolate ice cream and won a trophy for belching? Read all about it in *Lives of the Athletes*!

With the Author's Words

Once [Babe] Ruth was hospitalized for seven weeks following surgery for indigestion . . . said to be caused by a meal of twelve hot dogs and eight bottles of soda. He amazed companions with his wide throat—he could drink a glass of liquid in one swallow, including whole ice cubes. He didn't mind his reputation for grossness and sometimes overate just to add to the legend—ordering six sandwiches at a time or omelets made from eighteen eggs. (p. 20)

Babe Ruth was a legend in baseball . . . and in dining! Find out more quirky details about Babe and others in *Lives of the Athletes*.

Literature Extensions/Alternative Book Report Activities

Math/Economics—At Babe Ruth's peak, he was making $80,000 a year—more than four times what the next-highest-paid player was getting and more than Herbert Hoover, the president at that time. Salaries for many of today's athletic superheroes are astronomical, particularly when compared to the current president's salary! Students can research and debate this topic of salary levels in addition to other economics and sports issues, such as franchises, new stadiums and costs to fans, ticket prices, collective bargaining, strikes, and so on.

Informative books include *Baseball Economics: Current Research,* edited by John Fizel, et al. (Praeger Publishers, 1996); *Pay Dirt: The Business of Professional Team Sports* by James Quirk and Rodney D. Fort (Princeton University Press, 1997); and *Loser Takes All: Bud Adams, Bad Football, & Big Business* by Ed Fowler (Longstreet Press, 1997).

Government/Title IX/Women & Sports/Current Events/Internet—It is not surprising that only six of the twenty entries feature female athletes. Those entries give a realistic picture of the difficult times women have had becoming accepted as bona fide athletes, regardless of how skilled and talented they are in their sport. In an effort to make athletic opportunities equal for women, the government passed Title IX in 1972.

What does Title IX encompass? Begin a study by looking at the University of Iowa's "Gender Equity in Sports" at http://www.arcade.uiowa.edu/proj/ge/ and their "History of Title IX" timetable at http://www3.arcade.uiowa.edu/proj/ge/history.html, as well as the University of Texas's "WWW Women's Sports Page" at http://fiat.gslis.utexas.edu/~lewisa/womsprt.html. After general research, consider focusing student attention on the success (or lack of success) in implementing Title IX in the high schools and universities of your area.

History/Olympics/Internet—Many of the twenty athletes featured participated in the Olympics. Use this book and the picture of Zeus on the pre-title page to launch a study of the Olympic Games. Topics for consideration include the role of the Greek gods in the ancient games, the ancient games themselves, the modern games, how sites are selected, and the like.

Begin an Internet exploration with a visit to Tufts University's "Perseus Project" at http://olympics.tufts.edu/, which includes "Ancient and Modern Olympic Sports" and "A Tour of Ancient Olympia." With the alternating of the winter and summer games every two years, students can search for the official Web-sites for specific games, such as the XIX Olympic Winter Games in Salt Lake City, Utah, in the year 2002.

Writing/Biographies/Surveys/Research/Art—Have students survey a selected number of adults and students to compile a list of the best twenty contemporary athletes, excluding any included in *Lives of the Athletes*. Emulating Krull's unique format, students (in groups or individually) can research, write, lay out, and illustrate a book featuring the top twenty vote-getters. Students who feel less than comfortable with their artistic talents should be encouraged to doctor photographs and create collages to represent the athletes.

Bind the book and keep it in your classroom until the end of the year. Then donate it to the library so your young authors can have access to it in the years to come.

What the Neighbors Thought!

Books by Kathleen Krull

Lives of the Athletes: Thrills, Spills (And What the Neighbors Thought)

Lives of the Musicians: Good Times, Bad Times (And What the Neighbors Thought)

Lives of the Writers: Comedies, Tragedies (And What the Neighbors Thought)

Marcia Molina and the Days of the Dead

Wilma Unlimited: How Wilma Rudolph Became the World's Fastest Woman

Collective Biographies

Archer, Jules. *Breaking Barriers: The Feminist Revolution from Susan B. Anthony to Margaret Sanger to Betty Friedan*

Potter, Joan. *African Americans Who Were First*

Rappaport, Doreen. *Escape from Slavery: Five Journeys to Freedom*

Rappaport, Doreen. *Living Dangerously: American Women Who Risked Their Lives for Adventure*

Sinnott, Susan. *Extraordinary Asian Pacific Americans*

Stanley, Phyllis M. *American Environmental Heroes*

Thomas, Paul. *Campaigners (Rebels with a Cause)*

Picture the World of Sports!

Adler, David. *Lou Gehrig: The Luckiest Man*

Burleigh, Robert. *Hoops*

Golenbock, Peter. *Teammates*

Hall, Donald. *When Willard Met Babe Ruth*

Krull, Kathleen. *Wilma Unlimited: How Wilma Rudolph Became the World's Fastest Woman*

Mochizuki, Ken. *Baseball Saved Us*

Paulsen, Gary. *Dogteam*

Say, Allen. *El Chino*

Schwartz, David M. *Supergrandpa*

Shannon, David. *How Georgie Radbourn Saved Baseball*

Wilbur, Richard. *A Game of Catch*

London, Jonathan

Where's Home?

LC 94-39237. 1995. 89p. $13.99 (ISBN 0-670-86028-X). Viking. 1997. 96p. $3.99pa. (ISBN 0-140-37513-9pa.). Puffin.

Genre: Contemporary realistic fiction

Themes: Homelessness, home, imagination, fathers and sons, hitchhiking, mental illness, compassion, demonstrations, writing, unemployment, Vietnam vets, jail, juvenile justice system, migrant labor, fires, music, dance, San Francisco

Reading level: Fourth grade

Interest level: Fifth through tenth grade

Reviews:
Booklist. 91(19/20):1771 June 1/15, 1995.
Bulletin of the Center for Children's Books. 49(2):61 October 1995.
Kliatt Paperback and Audio Book Guide. 31(6):8 November 1997.
Publisher's Weekly. 242(30):66 July 24, 1995.
School Library Journal. 41(8):154 August 1995.

Author Information

A writer for children since 1989, Jonathan London has created picture books, retold Native American legends, and contributed poems and short stories to children's magazines. A traveler and a poet, London says his stories for children come from his experiences as a parent to his two sons. "I told them stories, both to put them to sleep and to wake them up." *Where's Home?* is London's first young adult novel.

Plot Summary

Fourteen-year-old Aaron has what his dad calls his "magination," but not much else. After Aaron's mentally ill mother leaves, his father's business fails, and they lose everything. He and his father have plans of starting over in San Francisco, and so they hitchhike West. Aaron is constantly hungry, misses his friends, and longs for a home.

Introducing the Book

Read aloud some of the following picture books about homelessness to introduce *Where's Home?* to your students: *Way Home* by Libby Hathorn (Crown, 1994); *Space Travellers* by Margaret Wild (Scholastic, 1993); or *Fly Away Home* by Eve Bunting (Clarion Books, 1991). The topic of homelessness combined with the book's wide margins, appealing typeface, and minimal number of pages will certainly appeal to reluctant readers.

Booktalks

On the Spot

Aaron is homeless and hungry. Will hitchhiking to California solve his problems?

With the Author's Words

Aaron and his father are homeless and have hitchhiked across much of the country to San Francisco. While his father is job hunting and looking through newspapers at the library, Aaron . . .

> traced our cross-country trip in a Hammond World Atlas. Wish we could have stopped at the Little Bighorn, Custer's Last Stand. At the end of the road, between two pages for California, I found a postcard slipped in there like a bookmark. Picture of a cable car climbing a steep hill. Flipped it over and it was blank. Figured I could send this to Hoops or Jelly back in the Big D. Say, "Wish you were here, ha-ha!" I decided to wait till I had a return address, and could afford a stamp. I didn't know my address would soon be 375 Woodside. A locked cell. (p. 27, hardback edition)

Is being homeless a crime? *Where's Home* for Aaron?

Literature Extensions/Alternative Book Report Activities

Current Events/Creative Writing—Aaron keeps a journal of sorts, writing down his hopes and dreams. Much of the content deals with the topic of "home." *Home* by Michael J. Rosen (HarperCollins, 1992) features seventeen illustrators and thirteen authors who celebrate the people and things that make up a home. Proceeds from the sale of this book support the nonprofit organization Share Our Strength's (SOS) fight against homelessness and hunger. Share this book with students to inspire their own essays about what home means to them.

Current Events/Vietnam Veterans/Internet—Aaron's dad and many of the other men they meet are Vietnam veterans who feel disenfranchised—struggling with homelessness, hunger, unemployment, or marginal employment. Books that focus on the return of Vietnam veterans and how they were treated by the public may help today's students understand more about these problems. Books to consider include *Three Faces of Vietnam* by Richard L. Wormser (Franklin Watts, 1993) and *Homecoming: When the Soldiers Returned from Vietnam* by Bob Greene (Perigee Books, 1989).

The Vietnam War Memorial has been helpful in healing some of these wounds. Eve Bunting's picture book *The Wall* (Clarion Books, 1990) is a tribute to Vietnam veterans and features mementos left at the wall. The first memento to appear at the memorial was a Purple Heart tossed into the wet cement of the foundation. Since then, more than 30,000 offerings have been left in tribute to those who died in Vietnam. The National Park Service has collected, preserved, and catalogued every item. *Offerings at the Wall* (Turner Publishing, 1995) lists each of the 58,183 names engraved as well as the mementos. Also visit "Vietnam Veterans Memorial" at http://www.nps.gov/vive/index2.htm.

Literature/Current Events/Homelessness—Picture books for older readers can easily be used to introduce topics for discussion or further study. Individually or in groups, students can study the homeless situation in your community. They can collect local statistics, visit a homeless shelter or foodbank and offer help, and present their findings to the class.

Encourage them to read aloud some of the following picture books to offer other perspectives on this topic: *Fly Away Home* by Eve Bunting (Clarion Books, 1991); *Ophelia's Shadow Theatre* by Michael Ende (Overlook Press, 1989); *This Home We Have Made, Esta Casa Que Hemos Hecho* by Anna Hammond and Joe Matunis (Crown, 1993); *Broken Umbrellas* by Kate Spohn (Viking, 1994); *Way Home* by Libby Hathorn (Crown, 1994); *Space Travellers* by Margaret Wild (Scholastic, 1993); and *We Are All in the Dumps with Jack and Guy: Two Nursery Rhymes with Pictures,* illustrated by Maurice Sendak (HarperCollins, 1993).

Social Issue/Migrant Workers—For a time, Aaron and his father travel throughout northern California finding work as migrants on farms. The stories in picture books for older readers can enhance an understanding of the issues migrant workers face—minimum wages, poor housing, and lack of food and education. Picture books to introduce these topics include *Radio Man: A Story in English and Spanish* by Arthur Dorris (HarperCollins, 1993); *Working Cotton* by Sherley Anne Williams (Harcourt Brace Jovanovich, 1992); *A Day's Work* by Eve Bunting (Clarion Books, 1994); and *Amelia's Road* by Linda Jacobs Altman (Lee & Low Books, Inc., 1993).

The following nonfiction books provide more information for discussion and research: *Voices from the Field: Children of Migrant Farm Workers Tell Their Stories* by S. Beth Atkin (Little, Brown and Company, 1993); *Dark Harvest: Migrant Farmworkers in America* by Brent Ashabranner (Linnet Books, 1997); *Kids at Work: Lewis Hine and the Crusade Against Child Labor* by Russell Freedman (Clarion Books, 1994); and *Cheap Raw Material* by Milton Meltzer (Viking, 1994).

Fathers & Sons

Carter, Alden R. *Wart, Son of Toad*

Cormier, Robert. *I Am the Cheese*

Crutcher, Chris. *Running Loose*

Griffin, Adele. *Sons of Liberty*

Haynes, David. *Right by My Side*

Koertge, Ron. *The Boy in the Moon*

London, Jonathan. *Where's Home?*

Myers, Walter Dean. *Somewhere in the Darkness*

Naylor, Phyllis. *The Keeper*

Spiegelman, Art. *Maus: A Survivor's Tale*

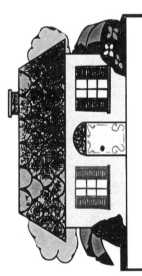

Where's Home?
Fact & Fiction

Artenstein, Jeffrey. *Runaways: In Their Own Words: Kids Talking About Living on the Streets*

Cwayna, Kevin. *Knowing Where the Fountains Are: Stories and Stark Realities of Homeless Youth*

Fox, Paula. *Monkey Island*

Grant, Cynthia D. *Mary Wolf*

Greenberg, Keith Elliot. *Runaways*

London, Jonathan. *Where's Home?*

Nelson, Theresa. *The Beggar's Ride*

Stavsky, Lois, and I. E. Mozeson. *The Place I Call Home: Faces and Voices of Homeless Teens*

Switzer, Ellen. *Anyplace but Here: Young, Alone, and Homeless: What to Do*

Talbot, Bryan. *The Tale of One Bat Rat*

Tough Times
for Tough
Kids

Cormier, Robert. *We All Fall Down*

Crutcher, Chris. *Staying Fat for Sarah Byrnes*

Deem, James M. *The 3 NBs of Julian Drew*

Draper, Sharon M. *Forged by Fire*

Johnston, Julie. *Adam and Eve and Pinch-Me*

Krisher, Trudy. *Spite Fences*

London, Jonathan. *Where's Home?*

Lynch, Chris. *Shadow Boxer*

Naidoo, Beverley. *No Turning Back: A Novel of South Africa*

Rottman, S. L. *Hero*

Thomas, Rob. *Rats Saw God*

Naidoo, Beverley

No Turning Back: A Novel of South Africa

LC 96-28980. 1995. 189p. $14.95 (ISBN 0-06-027505-7). HarperCollins. 1997. $4.99pa. (ISBN 1-85-978250-4pa.). HarperTrophy.

Genres: Contemporary realistic fiction, multicultural

Themes: South Africa, society, families, postapartheid, changes, street children, gangs, violence, abuse, survival, self-reliance, hunger, trust, peace, safety, begging, drug abuse, shelters, trust, education

Reading level: Fifth grade

Interest level: Fifth through tenth grade

Reviews:
Booklist. 93(3):342 October 1, 1996.
Bulletin of the Center for Children's Books. 50(6):217 February 1997.
Horn Book. 73(2):203 March/April 1997.
Voice of Youth Advocates. 20(2):246 October 1997. (#5 quality, #4 popularity)

Author Information

Born in Johannesburg, South Africa, Beverley Naidoo still resents the racist ignorance she suffered under as a child. When she was eighteen, Naidoo became aware of the significance of the racist structure of South African society. After college she began writing about the realities of South African life and how it was portrayed in children's books. Exiled to England because of her active participation against apartheid, Naidoo continues to write about the young people of South Africa.

Plot Summary

Twelve-year-old Sipho flees an abusive home life for a life on the streets of Johannesburg. The gang of street children he joins helps Sipho deal with constant hunger, cold nights, and loneliness. Yet who can Sipho trust in the postapartheid South African world of glue-sniffing gang members, police who harass kids, and white shop keepers who do not pay for work? Seeking peace and safety, Sipho takes a chance on a better life. The book includes a glossary of Zulu and African words.

Introducing the Book

The 189-page length (spread over 23 short chapters) is longer than most books of interest to reluctant readers. However, this reflection of the trials and travails of street children living on the edge of society will appeal to many. Capture the attention of potential readers by reading aloud to "And then he ran" (p. 2, hardback edition) or "A Gift from God: Being a Street Child" (p. xi, hardback edition), which is a poem by a previous street child who is now an assistant care worker at a shelter for homeless children.

Booktalks

On the Spot

What's worse? . . . living with an abusive stepfather or trying to sleep through cold nights on the streets? Survival on the street for a kid means dealing with gangs, drugs, hunger, and violence—whether it's in the United States or in South Africa.

With the Author's Words

Sipho and his homeless friends huddled together against the cold and danger and slept until they were awakened abruptly by a group of police officers who threw them into a van.

> *Suddenly the van gave an enormous shudder, and Sipho found himself flung forward as it came to a bumping halt. He was the first to be grabbed as the door swung open. "Okay, vuilgoed! Rubbish*

like you can get a nice wash here!" Ahead of him, glinting through the darkness, Sipho saw water. He screamed as he was picked up. He tried to struggle once again, but it was no use. The hands and arms were too powerful for him as they threw him out into the lake. Hitting, then breaking through the ice-cold water, his body shot out arms and legs in all directions. He couldn't swim. (p. 72, hardback edition)

There's *No Turning Back* for Sipho, and you'll have to read his story to discover his future.

Literature Extensions/Alternative Book Report Activities

Government/Democracy/Voting—While traveling on the bus to Johannesburg, Sipho overheard this hopeful conversation: "Let's hope the elections will bring us peace, Mama. When everyone makes their cross on the paper, there should be no need for fighting anymore" (p. 10, hardback edition). In conjunction with *No Turning Back*, read aloud both *The Day Gogo Went to Vote* by Elinor Batezar Sisulu (Little, Brown and Company, 1996), an uplifting story about the historic 1994 democratic elections in South Africa, and *You Want Women to Vote, Lizzie Stanton?* by Jean Fritz (Putnam Publishing Group, 1995) about the women's suffrage movement in the United States.

Use these books to launch a study of democracy, elections, and voting. Conduct a class or school election with proper nominations, speeches, debates, *Meet the Press*-type forums, campaigning, posters and banners, registering voters, ballots, polling places, and so forth.

Government/Exile—Because author Beverley Naidoo was actively involved in the movement against apartheid, she was exiled from South Africa. Many students will be fascinated with that fact. Encourage students to discover what living in exile really means. Enlightening books include *The Oxford Book of Exile,* edited by John Simpson (Oxford University Press, 1995); *Altogether Elsewhere: Writers on Exile,* edited by Marc Robinson (Harvest Books, 1996); *Artists Against Hitler: Persecution, Exile, Resistance,* edited by Gerhard Schoenberner (Inter Nationes, 1984); and *Border Crossings: Emigration and Exile* by Roger Rosen and Patra McSharry (Rosen Publishers Group, 1992).

History/Government/Democracy—Compare and contrast South Africa's struggle for democracy with the United States' struggles over slavery and civil rights. Helpful information about South Africa can be found in "South Africa Beyond Apartheid" in *Book Links* 3(3):33–38 January 1994 and *Against Borders: Promoting Books for a Multicultural World* (ALA Books, 1993), both by Hazel Rochman.

Sociology/Street Children/Current Events—Life is precarious and dangerous for the millions of children living on streets around the world. *No Turning Back* highlights the plight of these children in South Africa, but they also exist in Brazil, Egypt, Mexico, India, Thailand, the United States, and so forth. Are there homeless children in your community? What programs are in place for them? Working in groups or individually, students can investigate this situation locally, gather statistics, donate time at a local food bank or shelter, and report back to the entire class.

Helpful resources include *Lost Futures: Our Forgotten Children* by Stan Grossfeld (Aperture, 1997); *Amazing Grace: The Lives of Children and the Conscience of a Nation* by Jonathan Kozol (Crown, 1995); and articles discovered in periodical and Internet searches.

Reading 'Round the World

Africa
Dickinson, Peter. *AK*

Naidoo, Beverley. *No Turning Back: A Novel of South Africa*

Thailand
Ho, Minfong. *Rice Without Rain*

Israel
Nye, Naomi Shibab. *Habibi*

Germany
Lutzeier, Elizabeth. *The Wall*

Pakistan
Staples, Suzanne Fisher. *Haveli*

Staples, Suzanne Fisher. *Shabanu*

Japan
Watkins, Yoko Kawashima. *My Brother, My Sister, and I*

South Africa

Beake, Lesley. *The Song of Be*

Cased, Dianne. *92 Queens Road*

Gordimer, Nadine. *My Son's Story*

Gordon, Sheila. *Waiting for the Rain*

Isadora, Rachel. *At the Crossroads*

Maartens, Marita. *Paperbird*

Naidoo, Beverley. *Chain of Fire*

Naidoo, Beverley. *Journey to Jo'burg*

Naidoo, Beverley. *No Turning Back: A Novel of South Africa*

Rochman, Hazel, editor. *Somehow Tenderness Survives: Stories of Southern Africa*

Sacks, Margaret. *Beyond Safe Boundaries*

Sisulu, Elinor Batezar. *The Day Gogo Went to Vote*

Williams, Michael. *Crocodile Burning*

Street Kids Around the World

Bunting, Eve. *December*

Fox, Paula. *Monkey Island*

Hathorn, Libby. *Way Home*

Holtwijk, Ineke. *Asphalt Angels*

Luger, Harriett. *Bye, Bye, Bali Kai*

Mikaelson, Ben. *Sparrow Hawk Red*

Naidoo, Beverley. *No Turning Back: A Novel of South Africa*

Nelson, Theresa. *The Beggar's Ride*

Talbot, Bryan. *The Tale of One Bad Rat*

We Are All in the Dumps with Jack and Guy: Two Nursery Rhymes with Pictures. Illus. by Maurice Sendak

Pellowski, Michael Morgan

The Art of Making Comic Books

illustrated by
Howard Bender

LC 94-27589. 1995. 80p. $14.96 (ISBN 0-822-52304-3). Lerner Publications. 1995. 80p. $8.95 pa. (ISBN 0-822-59672-5 pa.). Lerner Publications.

Genres: Nonfiction, comics

Themes: Comics, imagination, artists, writers, book production, bookmaking, cartooning, cartoons, superheroes

Reading level: Sixth grade

Interest level: Fourth through twelfth grade

Reviews:
> *Booklist.* 92(9/10):826 January 1/15, 1996.
> *Bulletin of the Center for Children's Books.* 49(6):200 February 1996.
> *School Library Journal.* 42(1):122 January 1996.

Author Information

Born in New Jersey, Michael Morgan Pellowski received an athletic scholarship to attend Rutgers University, where he earned a degree in education and played baseball and football. Writing became his livelihood in 1975 (after he was unsuccessful in the NFL and CFL football drafts!), and Pellowski has written sports books, children's books, and worked for Archie Comics, Charlton Comics, Marvel Comics, and DC Comics. The four Pellowski offspring all like to read, write, and draw comics.

Plot Summary

This introduction to comic book production includes a historical overview, an explanation of jobs in large comic book companies, and an in-depth look at the "how" of comic book creation. Specifics include the visual and written development of character, plot, and setting; book format, panels, and layouts; the writing process, including story line, boxed captions, and dialogue balloons; and the art of drawing, with information about practice, equipment, and layout. The work includes a glossary, an index, and a bibliography.

Introducing the Book

Resist prejudices against comics and their worth, because this book has great appeal to kids who either love comics, who are curious about comic book production, or who are budding comic creators. Read aloud the first paragraph in the introduction (p. 7, either edition), then watch the copies zoom off the shelves! Zip! Zap! The perfect companion book (and very helpful for developing an understanding of the medium) is the renowned *Understanding Comics: The Invisible Art* by Scott McCloud (Kitchen Sink Press, 1994).

Booktalks

On the Spot

Zoom! Pow! Zap! Welcome to the world of comics! If you like to read them, or want to write or illustrate them, this is the book for you!

With the Author's Words

> Creating a character is your chance to let your imagination run wild . . . comic book stars have ranged from polite do-gooders to off-the-wall or imperfect folks with acne, hang-ups, and even money problems. Experiment with the absurd. Go one step beyond. The comic book field knows no boundaries where heroes and stars are concerned. (p. 25, either edition)

Literature Extensions/Alternative Book Report Activities

Art/Book Production—Students with limited artistic talent may be frustrated making their own comic books, but all students can explore and learn more about book production. The following books are guides for book-making activities for everyone: *From Pictures to Words: A Book About Making a Book* by Janet Stevens (Holiday, 1995); *Bookworks: Making Books by Hand* by Gwenyth Swain and the Minnesota Center for Book Arts (Carolrhoda, 1995); *Pop-O-Mania: How to Create Your Own Pop-Ups* by Barbara Valenta (Dial/Penguin, 1997); and *How to Make Pop-Ups* (William Morrow & Company, 1986) and *How to Make Super Pop-Ups*, both by Joan Irvine (Morrow/Beech Tree, 1992).

Since 1993, *Make Your Own Books: A Complete Kit* has been available from Running Press. More information about bookmaking for teachers and librarians can be found in the article "From Author's Chair to Bookmaker's Studio" by Richard F. Abrahamson and Betty Carter in *Book Links* 7(3):16–18 January 1997.

Art/Comics & Cartoons—Resources to help budding cartoonists and to complement *The Art of Making Comic Books* include *Understanding Comics: The Invisible Art* by Scott McCloud (Kitchen Sink Press, 1994); *How to Be a Successful Cartoonist* by Randy Glasbergen (North Light Books, 1996); and *Funny Papers: Behind the Scenes of the Comics* by Elaine Scott (William Morrow & Company, 1993). To help kids with actual drawings, provide such books as *Cartooning for Kids* by Marge Lightfoot (Owl Communications, 1993); *The Usborne Complete Book of Drawing* by Nigel Reece, et al. (EDC Publications, 1994); *Animation: How to Draw Your Own Flipbooks, and Other Fun Ways to Make Cartoons Move* by Patrick Jenkins (Kids Can Press, 1991); and numerous other drawing manuals.

Comics/Internet—There are many great comic sites for kids on the Internet. The "Internet Public Library" has a section on comics for teens at http://www.ipl.org/cgi-bin/teen/teen.db.out.pl?id=ae3000. Links to dozens of comic strips (including *Batman, Dark Knight, Bloom County, Calvin and Hobbes, Dilbert,* and *Peanuts*) are located at the "The Comic Strip" at http://www.unitedmedia.com/comics/, which includes archived cartoons, cartoonist biographies, profiles of comic characters, and a depiction of a future artist doodling his way through Public School 38.

Hobbies/Comics—Although most students don't have collector's editions, many kids have comic collections. Arrange a comic book swap. Invite a comic book "expert" and provide information about just how valuable some comics can become. Books such as *Collecting Comic Books: A Young Person's Guide* by Thomas S. Owens (Millbrook Press, 1995) include a general history, information about content and condition of comics, what to expect at comic shops, and the value of collecting free and inexpensive collectibles. Even though comic store personnel say there are many young comic buyers, basic collecting guides are geared for the typical comic reader, a twenty-one-year-old male. However, the most current edition of *The Overstreet Comic Book Price Guide* by Robert M. Overstreet (Avon), along with a current "price guide" periodical, will give students information they may be seeking.

How To?

The Art of Hand Reading by Lori Reid

The Art of Making Comic Books by Michael Morgan Pellowski

50 Nifty Ways to Earn Money by Andrea Urton

How to Do Homework Without Throwing Up by Trevor Romain

How to Haunt a House for Halloween by Robert Friedhoffer

How to Make Pop-Ups by Joan Irvine

How to Make Super Pop-Ups by Joan Irvine

Science Experiments You Can Eat by Vicki Cobb

What's Your Story? by Marion Dane Bauer

You Can Make Books Too!

Irvine, Joan. *How to Make Pop-Ups*

Irvine, Joan. *How to Make Super Pop-Ups*

Make Your Own Books: A Complete Kit

Stevens, Janet. *From Pictures to Words: A Book About Making a Book*

Swain, Gwneyth, and the Minnesota Center for Book Arts. *Bookworks: Making Books by Hand*

COMIC LOVERS

Avi. *City of Light, City of Dark*

Davis, Jim. *Garfield* series

Delgado, Ricardo. *Age of Reptiles: Tribal Warfare*

Feiffer, Jules. *The Man in the Ceiling*

Herge, Henge. The Adventures of *Tintin* series

Larson, Gary. *Far Side* series

Smith, Jeff. *Bone: Out from Boneville*, vol. 1

Smith, Jeff. *Bone: The Great Cow Race*, vol. 2

Watterson, Bill. *Calvin and Hobbes* series

Wenzel, David. *The Hobbit: Or There and Back Again*

Park, Barbara

Mick Harte Was Here

LC 94-27272. 1995. 90p. $15.00 (ISBN 0-679-87088-1); Alfred A. Knopf. 1996. $4.95pa. (ISBN 0-679-88203-0). Bullseye/Random House. 2 cassettes. 1997. $16.98 (ISBN 0-807-27796-7). Listening Library.

Genres: Contemporary realistic fiction, humor

Themes: Death, grief, accidents, brothers and sisters, friendship, bicycle safety, family life, head injuries, memories, feelings, funerals, cremation

Reading level: Fourth grade

Interest level: Fourth through eighth grade

Reviews:
The Book Report. 14(2):40 September/October 1995. (Recommended)
Booklist. 91(13):1242 March 1, 1995.
Bulletin of the Center for Children's Books. 48(10):356 June 1995. (Recommended)
Publishers Weekly. 242(9):104 February 27, 1995.
School Library Journal. 41(5):109 May 1995. (Starred review)

Author Information

Barbara Park was born in New Jersey but now lives in Phoenix, Arizona, with her husband and her children, who keep her aware of current trends. She likes writing for children because kids are not uptight; they enjoy laughing about themselves, and they appreciate the humor in her books. She considers herself the kind of children's author who never got over being a child. Park was a class clown and loved to make people laugh.

Plot Summary

Devastated by the bicycle accident that killed her brother Mick, thirteen-year-old Phoebe remembers his terrific sense of humor and funny pranks. Her memories and the recollected stories help Phoebe and her parents deal with Mick's death.

Introducing the Book

The first-person narrative, really funny stories, and tragic death will make this book an easy sell. In addition to the booktalks, consider reading aloud the first section of chapter 1, ending with "I just thought that would be fair" (p. 4, hardback edition) to entice readers.

Booktalks

On the Spot

Mick Harte was quite a character, and Phoebe is bound and determined no one will ever forget that he lived. Because, you see, Mick Harte is dead.

With the Author's Words

Phoebe—talking about her brother Mick.

> *The first big 'caper' we pulled together was right after Mick started kindergarten. That was when we defaced our first property. To be specific we scratched the letters F-A-R-T in the new driveway that had just been poured next to our house. We didn't do it to be bad. It's just that I was learning how to spell. And Mick was learning how to print. And the cement just sort of called to us, I guess you'd say. . . . All I remember is how excited we both were when he finished. We clapped, and jumped up and down, and totally laughed our heads off. Without a doubt, this was the funniest thing anyone had ever done in the entire history of the universe. It's amazing how a little fart in the driveway can totally lose its humor when your father sees it. (p. 12, hardback edition)*

Despite his recent death, these stories about Mick—his charm and his humor—can't help but make you laugh. And, you'll never forget that *Mick Harte Was Here*.

Literature Extensions/Alternative Book Report Activities

Psychology/Death and Dying/Grief/Funerals—Park does an excellent job of describing the stages of grief as she details Phoebe's reactions to Mick's death. Unfortunately in our society, adults and children are rarely prepared for coping with grief and death. Elizabeth Kübler-Ross wrote in her classic work *On Death and Dying* (Macmillan, 1969) that other than the fear of loud noises and of falling, many of our fears (like that of death) are learned responses. Provide books like the following to help students learn and understand more about death and grieving: *Corpses, Coffins, and Crypts* by Penny Colman (Henry Holt and Company, 1997); *The Kids' Book About Death and Dying by Kids for Kids* by Eric E. Rofes and the Unit at Fayerweather Street School (Little, Brown and Company, 1985); *Coping with Death and Grief* by Mary E. Heegaard (Lerner Publications, 1990); *Everything You Need to Know About Grieving* by Karen Spies (Rosen Publishers Group, 1990); *Part of Me Died, Too* by Virginia Lynn Fry (Dutton, 1995); and *Straight Talk About Death and Dying* by Robert Diguilio and Rachel Kranz (Facts on File, 1995). *Bereaved Children and Teens: A Support Guide for Parents and Professionals* (Beacon Press, 1995) is an excellent resource for adults who work with children.

Safety/Health/Internet/Bicycle Helmets—In the author's note at the end of this book, Barbara Park writes about bicycle accidents and how head injuries are the main cause of death in these cases. She says, "Researchers tell us that if all bicyclists wore helmets, as many as one death *every day* and one head injury every *four* minutes could be prevented." (p. 89, hardback edition)

This book provides an excellent springboard for a unit on bicycle safety. Invite an expert in to talk to students. Provide such resources as *A Kid's Guide to Staying Safe on Bikes* by Maribeth Boelts (Rosen Publishing Group, 1996); "Bicycle Helmet Safety Institute" at http://www.bhsi.org/; and "Bicycle Safety" at http://www.childsecure.com/bikes.htm, and "Night Bicycling" at http://www.childsecure.com/nitebike.htm at the "Child Secure" homepage.

Science/Insects/Flies/Internet—Mick's fixation about flies and their habits can inspire students to learn more about these insects. He would have loved *Old Black Fly* by Jim Aylesworth (Henry Holt and Company, 1992) with its splattered fly. Read it aloud to launch a discussion and a study. Other books are *The Housefly* by Heiderose Fischer-Nagel and Andreas Fischer-Nagel (Carolrhoda, 1990) and *Fly: A Read-About, Fold-Out, and Pop-Up* by David Hawcock (Random House, 1996), which describes the physical characteristics, reproductive process, eating habits, and behaviors of flies.

The following Websites are of interest: "House Fly" at http://hammock.ifas.ufl.edu/txt/fairs/8926, "How Far Can House Flies Fly?" at http://www.uky.edu/agriculture/entomology/entfacts/livestc/ef506.htm, and "Maryann Sterling's Art—Insects" at http://webclipart.miningco.com/msub11.htm.

Writing—Phoebe is determined not to forget Mick, and funny stories help to preserve her memories of him. Keeping track of memories is important, as Mick demonstrated when he collected photographs of his dog, Wocket, after the dog died. Mick stuck them "into the sides of his mirror to make sure he'd never forget" (p. 31, hardback edition).

Using picture book stories such as *Wilfred Gordon McDonald Partridge* by Mem Fox (Kane-Miller, 1989) and *The Memory Box* by Mary Bahr (Whitman, 1992) as models, students can collect, write about, and preserve memories. They may wish to select a pet, a relative, or friend. Some students may wish to share their memory collections; others may not.

Laughing All the Way:

Funny Stories

Blume, Judy. *Fudge-a-Mania*

Blume, Judy. *Superfudge*

Blume, Judy. *Tales of a Fourth Grade Nothing*

Byars, Betsy. Bingo Brown series

Cooper, Susan. *The Boggart*

Lowry, Lois. Sam series

Lynch, Chris. *Johnny Chesthair*

Manes, Stephen. *Be a Perfect Person in Just Three Days*

Naylor, Phyllis Reynolds. Alice series

Park, Barbara. *Mick Harte Was Here*

Paulsen, Gary. *Harris and Me*

Peck, Robert Newton. Soup series

Spinelli, Jerry. *Crash*

Park Yourself with Park: Great Reads by Barbara Park

Beanpole

Buddies

Dear God, Help!!! Love, Earl

Don't Make Me Smile

Junie B. Jones series

The Kid in the Red Jacket

Mick Harte Was Here

My Mother Got Married (And Other Disasters)

Operation: Dump the Chump

Rosie Swanson—Fourth Grade Geek for President

Skinnybones

Losing Someone: Death

Bauer, Marion Dane. *On My Honor*

Bohlmeijer, Arno. *Something Very Sorry*

Conly, Jane Leslie. *Crazy Lady!*

DeFelice, Cynthia. *The Apprenticeship of Lucas Whitaker*

Greene, Constance C. *Beat the Turtle Drum*

Henkes, Kevin. *Sun & Spoon*

Jukes, Mavis. *Blackberries in the Dark*

Lowry, Lois. *A Summer to Die*

Park, Barbara. *Mick Harte Was Here*

Paterson, Katherine. *Bridge to Terabithia*

Russell, Barbara T. *Last Left Standing*

Smith, Doris Buchanan. *A Taste of Blackberries*

VanOosting, James. *The Last Payback*

Yumoto, Kazumi. *The Friends*

Platt, Richard

Stephen Biesty's Incredible Explosions

illustrated by Stephen Biesty

LC 96-13948. 1996. 32p. $19.95 (ISBN 0-7894-1024-9). Dorling Kindersley.

Genre: Nonfiction

Themes: Construction, architecture, engineering, drawings, inventions, professions, science, geography, geology, history, physics, biology, archaeology, evolution, exploration, human body, space stations, windmills, hydraulics, perspective, transportation

Reading level: Sixth grade

Interest level: All ages

Reviews:
> *Publishers Weekly.* 243(32):440 August 5, 1996. (Starred review)
> *School Library Journal.* 42(10):138 October 1996.

Author Information

Stephen Biesty and Richard Platt are an amazing duo who together have published a series of "Incredible" books for Dorling Kindersley. Biesty has been a full-time illustrator since 1985. Platt went to art school after giving up a career as a civil engineer. He has been writing since 1980 and is a self-described "connoisseur of facts."

Plot Summary

Systematic drawings, with numerous tiny details and various points of view, reveal the inside and outside of twelve places, such as windmills, the Grand Canyon, a human body, a movie studio, the United States–Russia space station, and so forth. The fascinating drawings, looking like cross-sections of onion layers exploding in slow motion and frozen in time, are accompanied by short and snappy explanations. The work is indexed.

Introducing the Book

The use of double-page spreads, extended overleafs, and amusing details (the mill mice, sandwiches hidden under hats, and an alien hiding in each picture) invites readers to inspect this book carefully. To entice potential readers, point out some of these intriguing details or use the booktalks.

Booktalks

On the Spot

Did you know that scientists can't explain why we are unable to tickle ourselves? Or that the aircraft used to train astronauts was called the *Vomit Comet*? Or that recycled urine is sometimes used for cooking and drinking? You will if you take a look at these *Incredible Explosions*!

With the Author's Words

The facts:

> *If flying were as chaotic as driving, air travel would soon cease. (p. 12)*

> *In the most isolated spot on earth, the South Pole, the sun never sets in the summer, and winter is one long night. (p. 20)*

> *In the world of movies, nothing is quite what it seems. Buildings that seem to tower on screen are just tiny models. The giant squid dragging a ship beneath the waves is a latex puppet. (p. 22)*

A trip through the human body would be like surfing through the vast network of subways and sewers beneath a city. (p. 28)

Take an inside-outside tour of this airport, Antarctic base, movie studio, human body, and eight other places. The pictures in *Incredible Explosions* resemble cross-sections that seem to explode in slow motion and freeze in time.

Literature Extensions/Alternative Book Report Activities

Anatomy/Science/Book Collection—Use the "Human Body" section (pp. 28–29) as a unique introduction to anatomy. A collection of the following books fit well with Platt and Biesty's unusual perspective: *The Robot Zoo: A Mechanical Guide to the Way Animals Work* by John Kelly, Philip Whitfield, and Obin (Turner Publishing, 1994);"the scalpel-free guide to your insides" entitled *Brain Surgery for Beginners and Other Major Operations for Minors* by Steve Parker (Millbrook Press, 1993); and *How Dogs Really Work!* by Alan Snow (Little, Brown and Company, 1993).

History/Archaeologists—The "city cross-section" (pp. 16–19) looks back in time at eleven periods of human history with an archaeological perspective. The following picture books explore this same theme: *Under the Moon* by Dyan Sheldon (Dial Books for Young Readers, 1993); *The Backyard* by John Collier (Viking, 1993); *Home Place* by Crescent Dragonwagon (Macmillan, 1990); *The House on Maple Street* by Bonnie Pryor (William Morrow & Company, 1987); *Time Train* by Paul Fleischman (HarperCollins, 1991); and *Dreamplace* by George Ella Lyon (Orchard Books, 1993).

Focusing on your locale, students can research its history. What happened there 50, 100, 150, 200, 500, and 1,000 years ago? Presentations could be written, illustrated, or dramatized.

Physics/Bridges/Constructions/Contests/Internet—Biesty and Platt present exploded views of the Tower Bridge in London (pp. 26–27). Some schools, particularly high schools, participate in contests featuring the construction and testing of model bridges. Through cooperative learning, this activity promotes the study and application of the fundamental principles of physics.

Simple bridge building can be done in lower grades also. Using a proscribed number of popsicle sticks and wood glue, students can build bridges and have weight bearing contests. Consult the "Bridge Building Home Page" at http://www.iit.edu/~hsbridge/ for numerous ideas, including "Running Your Own School Bridge Contest."

Science/Energy/Wind/Alternative Power Sources—"The Windmill" (pp. 14–15) can help launch a study of the wind, how it moves things, and its potential as an alternative energy source. For more information about wind power, consult such books as *Energy All Around Us* by Donna Bailey (Raintree/Steck-Vaughn, 1991) and *Energy Resources: Towards a Renewable Future* by Margaret L. Madden (Franklin Watts, 1991).

The Wind at Work: An Activity Guide to Windmills by Gretchen Woelfle (Chicago Review Press, 1997) features both a history of windmills and more than a dozen wind-related activities. Consider having a kite contest as a cumulative activity celebrating the power of the wind.

Architecture

Adams, Robert. *Buildings: How They Work*

Architecture and Construction: Building Pyramids, Log Cabins, Castles, Igloos, Bridges, and Skyscrapers

Hussain, Iqbal. *Buildings*

Isaacson, Philip M. *Round Buildings, Square Buildings, & Buildings That Wiggle Like a Fish*

Macaulay, David. *Castle*

Macaulay, David. *Cathedral: The Story of Its Construction*

Macaulay, David. *City: A Story of Roman Planning and Construction*

Macaulay, David. *Great Moments in Architecture*

Macaulay, David. *Mill*

Macaulay, David. *Pyramid*

Macaulay, David. *Rome Antics*

Munro, Roxie. *Architects Make Zigzags: Looking at Architecture from A to Z*

Platt, Richard. *Stephen Biesty's Cross-Sections Castle*

Platt, Richard. *Stephen Biesty's Incredible Explosions*

Von Tscharner, Renata, and Ronald Lee Fleming. *New Providence: A Changing Cityscape*

Great Partners: Biesty and Platt

Platt, Richard. *Stephen Biesty's Cross-Sections: Castle*

Platt, Richard. *Stephen Biesty's Cross-Sections: Man-of-War*

Platt, Richard. *Stephen Biesty's Incredible Cross-Sections*

Platt, Richard. *Stephen Biesty's Incredible Everything*

Platt, Richard. *Stephen Biesty's Incredible Explosions*

Peek Beneath the Surface: Cross-Sections, Explosions . . .

Kelly, John, Philip Whitfield, and Obin. *The Robot Zoo: A Mechanical Guide to the Way Animals Work*

Macaulay, David. *Unbuilding*

Macaulay, David. *Underground*

Macaulay, David. *The Way Things Work*

Parker, Steve. *Brain Surgery for Beginners: And Other Major Operations for Minors*

Platt, Richard. *Stephen Biesty's Incredible Explosions*

Snow, Alan. *How Dogs Really Work!*

Polacco, Patricia
Pink and Say

LC 93-36340. 1994. unpaged. $16.95 (ISBN 0-399-22671-0). Philomel Books. 1997. VHS videotape. $44.99 (ISBN 6-304-28462-4). Saa Publishers.

Genres: Historical fiction, picture books, multicultural

Themes: Civil War, friendship, war, black soldiers, boy soldiers, death, fear, courage, deserters, hiding, heroism, war atrocities, slavery, survival, oral histories, reading, literacy, prisons

Reading level: Fourth grade

Interest level: Third grade and up

Reviews:
> *Booklist.* 91(1):54 September 1, 1994.
> *Bulletin of the Center for Children's Books.* 48(1):24 September 1994. (Recommended)
> *Horn Book.* 70(6):724–25 November/December 1994. (Starred review)
> *New York Times Book Review.* 144(49879):42 November 13, 1994.
> *Publishers Weekly.* 241(32):95 August 15, 1994.
> *School Library Journal.* 40(10):126–27 October 1994. (Starred review)

Author Information

Author/illustrator Patricia Polacco frequently draws on her own Russian and Irish heritage and her well-remembered childhood to create picture books. She spent school months in California and summers in Michigan and fondly remembers hearing older family members telling wonderful stories while she sat by the fire popping corn. For further information about Polacco, see the curriculum section below for an Internet author study.

Plot Summary

Left for dead, Say Curtis is rescued and befriended by Pinkus Aylee, who was separated from his black regiment. This Civil War story of two boy soldiers who were later imprisoned in Andersonville was passed down from generation to generation in Polacco's family.

Introducing the Book

This evocative picture book for older readers can be read aloud in its entirety, but the powerful illustrations need to be explored individually by students. Use this book in conjunction with any study of the Civil War, oral histories, or literacy.

Booktalks

On the Spot

(Show the double-page illustration of Pink and Say grasping hands on pp. 38–39.)

The two Civil War boy soldiers who are reading together on this book's cover are later wrenched apart after their capture. Read their story in Patricia Polacco's *Pink and Say*.

With the Author's Words

> *I know this story to be true because Sheldon Russell Curtis told his daughter, Rosa. Rosa Curtis Stowell told it to her daughter, Estella. Estella Stowell Barber, in turn, told it to her son, William. He then told me, his daughter, Patricia. When my father finished this story he put out his hand and said, "This is the hand, that has touched the hand, that has touched the hand, that shook the hand of Abraham Lincoln." (p. 42)*

This is the book about the hand of Civil War boy soldier Say and his friend Pink.

Literature Extensions/Alternative Book Report Activities

Drama/Readers' Theater/Internet—Access this short readers' theater script adaptation of *Pink and Say* at http://www.coe.ufl.edu/faculty/lamme/project/civilwar/sscivilwar.html. There are five speaking parts, including the narrator. Consult Aaron Shepard's "Readers on Stage: Tips for Reader's Theater" at http://www.aaronshep.com/rt/ROS.html for "an online guide to scripting, staging, and performing."

History/Black Soldiers/United States—*Pink and Say* is an excellent springboard for learning more about African Americans who have fought for the ideals of the United States. Provide books such as the following for a historical overview: *Black, Blue, & Grey: African Americans in the Civil War* by Jim Haskins (Simon & Schuster, 1997); *Black Heroes of the American Revolution* by Burke Davis (Harcourt Brace, 1992); *Undying Glory: The Story of the Massachusetts Fifty-Fourth Regiment* by Clinton Cox (Scholastic, 1993); *Hell Fighters: African American Soldiers in World War I* by Michael L. Cooper (Lodestar Books, 1997); *Lonely Eagles and Buffalo Soldiers: African Americans in World War II* by Tom McGowen (Franklin Watts, 1995); *Red-Tail Angels: The Story of the Tuskegee Airmen of World War II* by Patricia McKissack and Fredrick McKissack (Walker & Company, 1995); *The Tuskegee Airmen: Black Heroes of World War II* by Jacqueline L. Harris (Dillon Press, 1996); *Colin Powell: Soldier and Patriot* by Anne E. Schraff (Enslow, 1997); and *Colin Powell: Straight to the Top* by Rose Blue and Corinne J. Naden (Millbrook Press, 1997).

History/Slavery/Internet—Although students know about slavery in relation to the Civil War, many may not understand what slavery was really like prior to that time. Topics they can explore further include slave auctions, the breakup of families, living conditions, labor practices, punishment, education, and runaway slaves. Use this Internet lesson plan at http://ericir.syr.edu/plweb-cgi/fastweb?getdoc+ericir+ericir+4784+15+wAAA+oral%26history as a basis for exploring the history of slavery before the Civil War. Companion books include historical fiction such as *Ajeemah and His Son* by James Berry (Harpercrest, 1992) and *Nightjohn* by Gary Paulsen (Delacorte Press, 1993), in addition to informational books like *Christmas in the Big House, Christmas in the Quarters* by Patricia C. McKissack and Frederick L. McKissack (Scholastic, 1994); *A Williamsburg Household* by Joan Anderson (Clarion Books, 1988); *Dear Benjamin Banneker* by Andrea Davis Pinkney (Harcourt Brace and Company, 1994); and *The Strength of These Arms: Life in the Slave Quarters* by Raymond Bial (Houghton Mifflin, 1997).

Author Study/Polacco, Patricia/Internet—Polacco based *Pink and Say* on a family story passed down through generations. Many of Polacco's books are based on family events. Learn more about her and her family by reading *The Keeping Quilt* (Simon & Schuster, 1988); *The Bee Tree* (Philomel Books, 1993); and her autobiography, *Firetalking* (Richard C. Owen Publishing, 1994). Students can also investigate the Internet sites that feature Polacco, her books, and related activities: "Patricia Polacco: A Woman's Voice of Remembrance" at http://www.scils.rutgers.edu/special/kay/polacco.html; and "People in Books: Patricia Polacco Author, Illustrator, Storyteller" at http://www.ambook.org/bookweb/ab/0596/people.html.

WAR:
Small Books, BIG Trouble

Baillie, Allan. *Rebel*

Briggs, Raymond. *When the Wind Blows: The Story of the Bloggs and the Bomb*

Bunting, Eve. *Terrible Things: An Allegory of the Holocaust*

Emberley, Barbara. *Drummer Hoff*

Gauch, Patricia Lee. *Thunder at Gettysburg*

Heide, Florence Parry, and Judith Heide Gilliland. *Sami and the Times of the Troubles*

Innocenti, Roberto. *Rose Blanche*

Kodama, Tatsuharu. *Shin's Tricycle*

Lyon, George Ella. *Cecil's Story*

Morimoto, Junko. *My Hiroshima*

Polacco, Patricia. *Pink and Say*

Reeder, Carolyn. *Shades of Gray*

Seuss, Dr. *The Butter Battle Book*

Tsuchiya, Yukio. *Faithful Elephants: A True Story of Animals, People and War*

Turner, Ann. *Katie's Trunk*

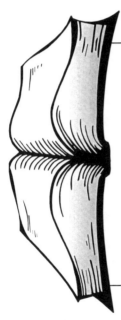

Power of Reading

Bradby, Marie. *More Than Anything Else*

DeClements, Barthe. *Sixth Grade Can Really Kill You*

Hahn, Mary Downing. *Daphne's Book*

Lasky, Kathryn. *Memoirs of a Bookbat*

Once Upon a Time: Celebrating the Magic of Children's Books

Paulsen, Gary. *Nightjohn*

Peck, Robert Newton. *Arly*

Polacco, Patricia. *Aunt Chip and the Great Triple Creek Dam Affair*

Polacco, Patricia. *The Bee Tree*

Polacco, Patricia. *Pink and Say*

Smith, Doris Buchanan. *The Pennywhistle Tree*

Spinelli, Jerry. *Maniac Magee*

Civil War Novel

Beatty, Patricia. *Jayhawker*

Clapp, Patricia. *The Tamarack Tree*

Collier, James Lincoln. *With Every Drop of Blood*

Fleischman, Paul. *Bull Run*

Forman, James. *My Enemy, My Brother*

Houston, Gloria. *Mountain Valor*

Hunt, Irene. *Across Five Aprils*

Hurmence, Belinda. *A Girl Called Boy*

Reeder, Carolyn. *Across the Lines*

Reeder, Carolyn. *Shades of Gray*

Rinaldi, Ann. *In My Father's House*

Shore, Laura. *The Sacred Moon Tree*

Steele, William. *The Perilous Road*

Wilson, Linda Miller. *Summer Spy*

Wisler, G. Clifton. *The Drummer Boy of Vicksburg*

Wisler, G. Clifton. *Red Cap*

Skurzynski, Gloria
Virtual War

LC 96-35346. 1997. 152p. $16.00 (ISBN 0-689-81374-0).
Simon & Schuster Books for Young Readers.

Genre: Science fiction

Themes: Futuristic life, war, virtual reality, genetic engineering, contamination, pollution, manipulation, concentration, trust, courage, mind control, teamwork, cooperation, decision making, loyalty, honesty, honor, self-confidence, obedience, horror of war, codes, reflexes, mutations, diversity, rules, computers

Reading level: Fifth grade

Interest level: Fifth through ninth grade

Reviews:
Booklist. 93(22):1891 August 1997.
Bulletin of the Center for Children's Books. 50(11):413 July/August 1997. (Recommended)
Publishers Weekly. 244(20):76 May 19, 1997.
School Library Journal. 43(7):98 July 1997.
Voice of Youth Advocates. 20(3):196 August 1997. (#5 quality, #4 popularity)

Author Information

Gloria Skurzynski grew up in a smoke-filled steel town in western Pennsylvania and now lives in Salt Lake City, Utah, where she writes fiction and nonfiction for young people. She is fascinated with "the wonderment of the world to come" and enjoys living in this age of amazing technology. "I only wish I could live forever, so I could see how the future turns out," she says. Yet Skurzynski is somewhat concerned about the future. She worries about the lack of imagination she sees in today's kids and feels they should be encouraged to create technology rather than just to consume its results. That's the theme of *Virtual War*—Corgan can only succeed when he learns to think on his own. Skurzynski's e-mail address is @ix.netcom.com, and she wants to receive letters from readers.

Plot Summary

The little bit of uncontaminated land left on earth in the year 2080 is priceless, and those who want it plan a virtual war to determine ownership. The soldiers who will fight this war are genetically engineered and have trained for fourteen years. For the Federation, the army consists of fourteen-year-old Corgan, a master of reaction and reflex; Sharla, a superlative code breaker; and Brig, a mutant strategic expert. These three have been isolated and in training for most of their young lives. Corgan, in particular, has never broken the rules and is committed to perform with bravery and honor no matter what the circumstances. Yet even though this war is only "virtual," it's horrible just the same.

Introducing the Book

Read chapter 1 aloud to acquaint readers with the futuristic world and the characters in this fast-paced novel. Repeat the pledge, "I promise to wage the War with courage, determination, and honor," at the end of the chapter. (p. 124, hardback edition) Be sure students know about the author's *Cyberstorm: A Novel with a Virtual Reality Twist* (Macmillan Books for Young Readers, 1995).

Booktalks

On the Spot

It's a Nintendo player's dream come true: nonstop, virtual reality war games designed to increase reflexes and improve timing. But when the war really begins—the fun stops.

With the Author's Words

Fourteen-year-old Corgan has led a strange life. Genetically engineered to have the best reflexes in the world, he has been carefully protected against everything—even other humans. But that is all about to change. . . .

It was going to happen, then. For the first time in his life, Corgan was going to touch a human being. He knew it would be dangerous, because contamination got spread by touch from person to person, which was why ninety-three percent of the Earth's human population had ceased to exist in the past eighty years. He'd been taught the danger ever since he could remember knowing anything, and now—he didn't care. (p. 29, hardback edition)

Literature Extensions/Alternative Book Report Activities

Current Events/Land Mines—The armies participating in the virtual war struggled to save their troops from land mines: "He kept having to choose . . . straight ahead the platoon might enter a minefield, where a dozen of [his troops] would get blown to pieces before he could move them out. Or the minefield might be to the left or to the right; planted at random, land mines were undetectable." (pp. 112–13, hardback edition)

Skurzynski's writing on this topic can serve as the segue to a current events discussion concerning land mines worldwide. Acquaint students with these 1997 events: 1) The Nobel Peace Prize was awarded to the International Campaign to Ban Land Mines and its American coordinator, Jody Williams of Vermont; 2) the United States continued its resistance to a global ban on the deadly devices despite 125 nations signing the agreement; and 3) the campaign to ban land mines received much attention after the death of Princess Diana of Great Britain, who was a champion of the cause.

Students can learn more about land mines by searching both the Internet and using traditional print resources. Focus on the history and use of land mines in different wars, where they are manufactured, clean-up efforts, injuries inflicted on citizens in times of peace, and why the U.S. government has been opposed to a global ban.

Science/Genetic Engineering/Cloning—Corgan and Sharla's talents are enhanced by genetic engineering, and Brig is a mutant as a result of genetic experiments. Recently, the world has learned about successful experiments in this field with news reports about Dolly, the Scottish sheep; the cloned cows in Wisconsin; and the monkeys in Oregon. This has been a futuristic topic of interest to many over the years. Is the future about to meet the present?

Books such as *Genetic Engineering: Progress or Peril?* by Linda Tagliaferro (Lerner Publications, 1997) and *Clone: The Road to Dolly and the Path Ahead* by Gina Kolata (William Morrow & Company, 1997) can help students understand the medical, political, theological, and ethical implications in this area of science.

Science/Senses/Touch—Corgan reached the age of fourteen before he had ever been touched by another human being. The first time Sharla made contact with him, "he trembled so violently that he almost fell against the wall" (p. 29, hardback edition). The bond this touch creates between Corgan and Sharla allows them to work successfully together and emphasizes the importance of touch in human development. There have been many studies centered on touch, from the classic work *Touching: The Human Significance of the Skin* by Ashley Montagu (Columbia University Press, 1971) to scientific studies that measure infant development and its relationship to being held. Students can learn more by reading *Touching* by Henry Arthur Pluckrose and Chris Fairclough (Gareth Stevens, 1995) and *Smell, Taste and Touch: The Sensory Systems* by Jenny Bryan (Dillon Press, 1994).

Science/Virtual Technology/Internet—The use of virtual reality in everyday life can be seen in the fast-growing market of computerized entertainment games. Many students will be interested in virtual tours on the Internet, whether or not they have access to commercial virtual entertainment centers. Take the following virtual tours: "Earth Science Explorer" at http://www.cotf.edu/ete/modules/msese/explorer.html, "Amazon Adventure" at http://vif27.icair.iac.org.nz/, "Virtual Renaissance: A Journey Through Time Travel" at http://www.osgo.ks.he.schule.de/Lichtenberg/Material/, "Virtual Frog Dissection Kit" at http://www.itg.lbl.gov/ITG.hm.pg.docs/dissect/info.html, and the National Air and Space Museum's "How Things Fly" at http://www.nasm.edu/GALLERIES/GAL109/.

Great SF for Middle Grades

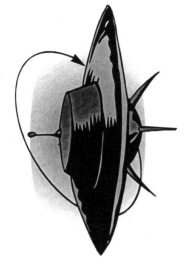

Dexter, Catherine. *Alien Game*

Hoover, H. M. *Away Is a Strange Place to Be*

Klause, Annette Curtis. *Alien Secrets*

Mahy, Margaret. *The Greatest Show off Earth*

Rubinstein, Gillian. *Skymaze*

Rubinstein, Gillian. *Space Demons*

Service, Pamela. *Weirdos of the Universe, Unite!*

Skurzynski, Gloria. *Virtual War*

Sleator, William. *Interstellar Pig*

It's All in Your Mind—ESP

Aaron, Chester. *Out of Sight, Out of Mind*

Belden, Wilanne S. *Mind-Hold*

DeClements, Barthe. *Double Trouble*

Duncan, Lois. *A Gift of Magic*

Gloss, Molly. *Outside the Gates*

Lunn, Janet. *Shadow in Hawthorn Bay*

Roberts, Willo Davis. *Girl with the Silver Eyes*

Sargent, Sarah. *Watermusic*

Service, Pamela. *Being of Two Minds*

Skurzynski, Gloria. *Virtual War*

Slepian, Jan. *The Mind Reader*

The World in Virtual Reality

Cross, Gillian. *New World*

Friesner, Esther. *The Sherwood Game*

Goldman, E. M. *The Night Room*

Jones, Diana Wynne. *Hexwood*

Kritlow, William. *A Race Against Time*

Skurzynski, Gloria. *Virtual War*

Skurzynski, Gloria. *Cyberstorm: A Novel with a Virtual Reality Twist*

Velde, Vivian Vande. *User Unfriendly*

Westwood, Chris. *Virtual World*

Temple, Frances

Grab Hands and Run

LC 92-34063. 1993. 164p. $14.95 (ISBN 0-531-05480-2). Orchard Books. 1995. 176p. $4.50pa. (ISBN 0-064-40548-6). HarperTrophy.

Genres: Contemporary realistic fiction, adventure, multicultural

Themes: Families, political oppression, refugees, freedom, survival, human rights, El Salvador, Salvadorans, totalitarianism, courage, fear, hope, safe houses, human rights, illegal aliens, emigration, borders, political refugees, soldiers, activists, escape, cultures, bribes, trust, betrayal, citizenship

Reading level: Fourth grade

Interest level: Fourth to eighth grade

Reviews:
Booklist. 89(17):1596 May 1, 1993. (Starred review)
Horn Book. 69(3):335 May/June 1993. (Starred review)
New York Times Book Review. 142(49403):29 July 25, 1993.
Publishers Weekly. 240(15):64 April 12, 1993. (Starred review)
School Library Journal. 39(4):143–44 April 1993. (Starred review)

Author Information

Frances Temple grew up all over the world—Virginia, France, and Vietnam. Stories surrounded her all her life, and she became particularly interested in writing about young people who survive terrible dangers. While living near the Canadian border, Temple's family sheltered a refugee family—a mother and two children whose father had been killed in El Salvador—until they could immigrate to Canada. *Grab Hands and Run* was based on this family's experiences. After five months with Temple's family, they settled in Canada, and later they took a trip back to El Salvador. Temple shared her publisher's advance with the family and financed this visit. Temple died suddenly of a heart attack in 1995.

Plot Summary

Fearing for their lives after the suspicious disappearance of their father, twelve-year-old Felipe, his younger sister, and their mother flee El Salvador for Canada. Their success depends on avoiding the authorities, bribing the right people, and relying on their own physical stamina and courage. The grueling journey hones their survival skills, but only luck, determination, and documentation will gain them status as political refugees after they are imprisoned in the United States as illegal aliens.

Introducing the Book

This authentic story is based on the accounts of a Salvadoran family who lived with the author's family while waiting for Canadian citizenship. The excitement of their dangerous journey will appeal to many readers, particularly boys and girls who like adventure and survival stories. To introduce the book, read aloud the family's rules for the road on page 44:

"Avoid the authorities, Be polite.
Let Mama do the talking.
Like a chameleon, blend in wherever you are."

Booktalks

On the Spot

Fearing for their lives, two kids and their mom flee their Central American home for safety and freedom in Canada. They *Grab Hands and Run*, but can they survive this illegal, dangerous, and grueling trip north?

With the Author's Words

(Prop: Write the note below in clumsy handwriting.)

It's hot in our yard. I'm happy to open the door to the house, which is built of concrete blocks and is always shady and cool. I see a piece of paper stuck under the door, just inside. I pick it up . . . I read the note while I'm going for a glass of water. . . .

LEAVE AND DON'T COME BACK. IF NOT, YOU DIE.

I wonder why they put the line under "you." I lean my forehead against the watercooler. There is nothing on the other side of the note. It's not addressed to anyone. (pp. 32–33, paperback and hardback editions)

But, Felipe's mother knows it's a death threat for her family. It's time to *Grab Hands and Run*. Read the story of their grueling trip through jungles, over rivers, and across the unknown.

Literature Extensions/Alternative Book Report Activities

Citizenship/Interviews/Internet—Felipe and his family suffered greatly from their government's oppression. When citizens grow up in a country with as many freedoms as those in the United States, they often don't appreciate their rights. What are the rights and responsibilities of citizenship? Arrange to have students attend a naturalization ceremony in your community. Have them interview these new citizens about what being a citizen of the United States means to them. For comparison, have students also interview citizens who were born in this country. Compile and discuss the results.

Consult the lesson plans and activities at the "Center for Civic Education" at http://www.civiced.org/lesson-plans.html for other ideas and information.

Cultural Diversity/Holidays/Day of the Dead—Felipe misses the Day of the Dead celebration (the Latino equivalent of Halloween) with the graveyard visits, special foods, and friends. Use books like *Days of the Dead* by Kathryn Lasky (Hyperion, 1996) and *Day of the Dead* by Tony Johnston (Harcourt Brace and Company, 1997) to learn more about the traditions of this three-day celebration held from October 31 to November 2. Consider including a Day of the Dead activity in a celebration of cultural diversity along with, or instead of, Halloween. Some communities stage parades and other festivities in conjunction with local arts groups.

Current Events/Government/Refugees/Internet—Felipe's family was not trying to settle in the United States. Their goal was to get to Canada, but they were caught and detained in the United States. What are the current immigration policies of the United States? What constitutes being a political refugee? Is admission still based on country-by-country allocations? What are the rates of deportation in the 1990s? Why are some U.S. citizens concerned about immigration? Search for answers to these and other questions on Internet news sites such as "Pathfinder" at http://pathfinder.com, *The New York Times* at http://www.nytimes.com, the "United States Immigration and Naturalization Service" at http://www.ins.usdoj.gov, and the extensive citizenship and immigration links provided by D. L. Hennessey at http://www.mindspring.com/~citizenship/links.html.

The following books can provide students with information about refugees and immigration: *Into a Strange Land* by Brent Ashabranner (Putnam Publishing Group, 1988); *Closing the Borders* by Wendy Davis (Thomson Learning, 1995); *One Day We Had to Run! Refugee Children Tell Their Stories in Words and Paintings* by Sybella Wilkes (Millbrook Press, 1995); and *United Nations High Commissioner for Refugees: Making a Difference in Our World* by Leslie Burger (Lerner Publications, 1996).

Current Events/Human Rights—After Felipe and his friend discover a human arm in a nearby empty lot, Felipe's father reports this to a human rights activist group. The United States and the world community are continually investigating occurrences of human rights violations in countries throughout the world. In addition, human rights groups in the United States work to report and eliminate hate crimes. Students can research statewide, regional, or national human rights groups and learn about their activities. For a global perspective, point students toward the Internet and periodical databases for current human rights activities.

Around the World: Political Conflict & Kids

Baillie, Allan. *Rebel*

Filipovic, Zlata. *Zlata's Diary: A Child's Life in Sarajevo*

Foreman, Michael. *War Boy: A Country Childhood*

Innocenti, Roberto. *Rose Blanche*

Jenkins, Lyll Becerra de. *The Honorable Prison*

Lowry, Lois. *Number the Stars*

Naidoo, Beverley. *Journey to Jo'burg*

Salisbury, Graham. *Under the Blood-Red Sun*

Sisulu, Elinor Batezar. *The Day Gogo Went to Vote*

Temple, Frances. *Grab Hands and Run*

Uchita, Yoshiko. *The Bracelet*

Latinos

Carlson, Lori M., and Cynthia L. Ventura, eds. *Where Angels Glide at Dawn: New Stories from Latin America*

Jenkins, Lyll Becerra de. *So Loud a Silence*

Jimenez, Francisco. *The Circuit*

Mazzio, Joann. *The One Who Came Back*

Mikaelson, Ben. *Sparrow Hawk Red*

Perera, Hilda. *Kiki: A Cuban Boy's Adventures in America*

Soto, Gary. *Baseball in April and Other Stories*

Soto, Gary. *Pacific Crossing*

Temple, Frances. *Grab Hands and Run*

Refugees: Escaping Danger

Beatty, Patricia. *Lupita Manana*

Bergman, Tamar. *Along the Tracks*

Bernardo, Anilu. *Jumping Off to Freedom*

Buss, Fran Leeper. *Journey of the Sparrows*

Hartling, Peter. *Crutches*

Hesse, Karen. *Letters from Rifka*

Hussein, Ikram. *Teenage Refugees from Somalia Speak Out*

Kawashima, Yoko. *So Far from the Bamboo Grove*

Laird, Elizabeth. *Kiss the Dust*

Shea, Pegi Deitz. *The Whispering Cloth: A Refugee's Story*

Temple, Frances. *Grab Hands and Run*

Whelan, Gloria. *Goodbye, Vietnam*

Tillage, Leon Walter

Leon's Story

LC 96-43544. 1997. 107p. $14.00 (ISBN 0-374-34379-9).
Farrar Straus & Giroux.

Genres: Biography, multicultural

Themes: Childhood, African Americans, race relations, segregation, survival, racism, violence, prejudice, poverty, family life, oral histories, sharecroppers, Civil Rights movement, Jim Crow laws, democracy, hopes and dreams, Ku Klux Klan, North Carolina, tobacco

Reading level: Fifth grade

Interest level: Fifth grade and up

Reviews:

Booklist. 94(3):332 October 1, 1997. (Starred review)

Horn Book. 73(6):699–700 November/December 1997. (Starred review)

Publishers Weekly. 244(37):77 September 8, 1997. (Starred review)

School Library Journal. 43(12):148 December 1997.

Author Information

Born into a sharecropper family near Fuquay, North Carolina, in 1936, Leon Walter Tillage was the second oldest of eight children. He remembers cursing his black skin color as a boy. His childhood, lived during years of segregation, overt racism, and cruelty to people of color, is a story of survival. Coming of age during the Civil Rights movement, Tillage was able to gain some control over his own life. He has worked at many jobs but has been a custodian at Park School in Baltimore for more than thirty years. A scholarship fund to help local kids, regardless of color, has been established in his name and was recognized by the Maryland House of Delegates. He is the father of three children.

Plot Summary

Tillage's recollections recall the difficult and frightening times he and his family (and most African Americans) lived through during the first half of the twentieth century. His story, transcribed by Susan Roth from tape-recorded interviews, reminds readers of a time not so long ago when many faced a world of segregation filled with hatred and racism. For Tillage, a future with choice and peace was possible only as a result of the Civil Rights movement in the 1960s. An afterword and a note about the book are included.

Introducing the Book

The small size of this book and the black-and-white photograph on the cover will provide immediate appeal to reluctant readers. In addition, this biography is short, with large typeface and ample white space. The ten sections are separated by pages of collage designs and patterns. To hook readers, read aloud "Leon," the first section (p. 3), or use the booktalks below. Students who resist those perennial biography assignments will snap this up with alacrity.

Booktalks

On the Spot

Diving down into a ditch to hide when school buses carrying white children drove by . . . watching your father killed by a carload of white teenagers . . . living a life filled with fear—this is all part of *Leon's Story*, a telling of growing up as a black child during years of segregation, prejudice, and violence.

With the Author's Words

I was afraid to walk the road at night because of the Klansmen. It was all dirt roads in those days. If I was walking down a road at night, I would constantly be looking behind me. If a car came, I automatically jumped down the embankment and hid in the ditch, or if it was a wooded area, I would run out in the woods and lay down and be real quiet, because if they caught me, they'd beat me up and hurt me, and they called it having fun. To them it was fun. . . . [Sometimes] we used to walk the rail-road track or walk the footpath at night in the woods at the edge of the fields so we wouldn't be seen out there in the open. If you did, you would really regret it. (pp. 56–57, hardback edition)

It's hard to believe this happened in the United States only sixty years ago. Yet for many African Americans, it is all too real, and their history is a study of survival. Leon Tillage is one of those survivors, and his story is something no one should ever forget.

Literature Extensions/Alternative Book Report Activities

Economics/Current Events/Health/Tobacco/Debate—Tillage helped his father grow tobacco, and he worked after school and at night unloading trucks at the tobacco market and worked around the warehouse. Tobacco was, and is, an important crop for the economy of the South.

Students can investigate any of a variety of issues concerning tobacco. Hot topics arising from the June 1997 government/tobacco companies agreement include: reducing teen smoking, FDA regulation, work-place smoking bans, antitobacco campaigns, and health concerns. Many of these topics lend themselves to the classic debate format. After students conduct research and collect data using periodical guides and data-bases, Internet sources, and the like, they should be prepared to argue either side.

History/Segregation/Martin Luther King, Jr./Internet—President Lincoln's 1863 Emancipation Proclama-tion declared all slaves "forever free." Yet in reality, most former slaves and their descendants lived in pov-erty and faced cruelty and scant opportunities. Indeed, many were harassed and tormented as Tillage reveals in his autobiography. For a long time, this was everyday life for African Americans following the Civil War. *Leon's Story* provides dramatic and realistic information to include with a study of the history of Civil Rights in the United States. Students can investigate any one of a variety of issues and topics, such as segre-gation, the Ku Klux Klan, Jim Crow laws, voting rights, and so on.

For information about the most important Civil Rights leader, Martin Luther King Jr., consult the fol-lowing books and Internet sites: *Martin Luther King* by Rosemary Bray (Mulberry Books, 1997); *The Life and Death of Martin Luther King Jr.* by James Haskins (Lothrop, 1997); *Let Freedom Ring: A Ballad of Martin Luther King, Jr.* by Myra Cohn Livingston (Holiday, 1992); *I Have a Dream* by Martin Luther King Jr. (Scholastic Press, 1997); "Martin Luther King, Jr.—American Civil-Rights Leader" at http://www.bena.com/lucidcafe/library/96jan/king.html; the virtual tour at the "National Civil Rights Mu-seum" at http://www.mecca.org/~crights/cyber.html; and "Martin Luther King Jr." at *The Seattle Times* site at http://www.seattletimes.com/mlk/.

Language Arts/History/Oral Histories/Internet—*Leon's Story* is an evocative and poignant oral history. Every person and family has a history, and when students participate in oral history projects they often dis-cover important and sometimes unusual things about family members. Develop a family history project for your class. For inspiration, see all or part of the ten-part PBS series *Ancestors*, which highlights the positive impact family histories can have on individuals. Visit the companion Internet site for the series at http://www.kbyu.byu.edu/ancestors.html for a schedule, a teacher's guide, and other helpful information.

For more assistance, access interview questions for collecting oral histories at http://www.rootsweb. com/~genepool/oralhist.htm at the "Rootsweb Genealogical Data Cooperative." An additional resource is *Keepsakes: Using Family Stories in Elementary Classrooms* by Linda Winston (Heinemann, 1997).

Language Arts/Oral Histories—*Leon's Story* is an oral history that comes from the heart of the teller's memo-ries. Tillage made an audio recording of his story for Susan Roth, the illustrator, who then transcribed the text from "that original tape and from two other tapes that were made later for clarification purposes." (p. 104, hardback edition) Roth's editing strove to maintain Leon's voice while "bridging the gap between the spoken and the written word." (p. 104) Tillage helped with and approved of all changes.

For more family histories, see the following picture books: Allen Say's autobiographical books include *Grandfather's Journey* (Houghton Mifflin, 1993); *The Bicycle Man* (Houghton Mifflin, 1982); and *Tree of Cranes* (Houghton Mifflin, 1991). Additional insights about his family can be found in his Caldecott medal acceptance speech for *Grandfather's Journey* (*Horn Book* 70[4]:427–31 July–August 1994). Likewise, some aspects of Patricia Polacco's family history are the basis for *Pink and Say* (Philomel Books, 1994); *The Bee Tree* (Philomel Books, 1993); *The Keeping Quilt* (Simon & Schuster, 1988); and others.

Oral history projects help build skills in reading, writing, and research. Use books like these as models for student projects: *I Was Dreaming to Come to America: Memories from the Ellis Island Oral History Project,* edited by Veronica Lawlor (Viking Children's Books, 1995); *Lasting Echoes: An Oral History of Native American People* by Joseph Bruchac (Harcourt Brace and Company, 1997); *Oh, Freedom! Kids Talk About the Civil Rights Movement with the People Who Made It Happen* by Casey King and Linda Barrett Osborne (Knopf/Borzoi, 1997); and *Freedom's Children: Young Civil Rights Activists Tell Their Own Stories,* edited by Ellen Levine (G. P. Putnam's Sons, 1993).

Real People, Real Stories: Biographies

Ashby, Ruth, and Deborah Gore Ohrn, eds. *Herstory: Women Who Changed the World*

Colman, Penny. *Rosie the Riveter*

Filipovic, Zlata. *Zlata's Diary*

Frank, Anne. *The Diary of a Young Girl: The Definitive Edition*

Freedman, Russell. *The Life and Death of Crazy Horse*

Sis, Peter. *Starry Messenger: A Book Depicting the Life of a Famous Scientist, Mathematician, Astronomer, Philosopher, Physicist, Galileo Galilei*

Stanley, Diane. *Leonardo Da Vinci*

Stanley, Diane. *Shaka: King of the Zulus*

Tillage, Leon Walter. *Leon's Story*

Stories of Growing Up Black: 1900–1965

Curtis, Christopher Paul. *The Watsons Go to Birmingham—1963*

Igus, Toyomi. *Going Back Home: An Artist Returns to the South*

Meyer, Carolyn. *White Lilacs*

Moore, Yvette. *Freedom Songs*

Nelson, Vaunda Micheaux. *Mayfield Crossing*

Robinet, Harriette Gillem. *Mississippi Chariot*

Taylor, Mildred D. *The Gold Cadillac*

Taylor, Mildred D. *Let the Circle Be Unbroken*

Taylor, Mildred D. *The Road to Memphis*

Taylor, Mildred D. *Roll of Thunder, Hear My Cry*

Taylor, Mildred D. *Song of the Trees*

Taylor, Mildred D. *The Well: David's Story*

Tillage, Leon Walter. *Leon's Story*

Wilkinson, Brenda. *Ludell*

The Real Lives of African Americans

Bernotas, Bob. *Spike Lee: Filmmaker*

Berry, S. L. *Langston Hughes*

Bray, Rosemary. *Martin Luther King*

Igus, Toyomi. *Going Back Home: An Artist Returns to the South*

McKissack, Pat, and Fredrick McKissack. *Red-Tail Angels: The Story of the Tuskegee Airmen of World War II*

McKissack, Pat, and Fredrick McKissack. *Sojourner Truth: A Voice for Freedom*

Meltzer, Milton. *Mary McLeod Bethune: A Voice of Black Hope*

Myers, Walter Dean. *Malcolm X: By Any Means Necessary*

Parks, Rosa, and Jim Haskins. *Rosa Parks: My Story*

Rutberg, Becky. *Mary Lincoln's Dressmaker: Elizabeth Keckley's Remarkable Rise from Slave to White House Confidante*

Sanford, William R. *Bill Pickett: African-American Rodeo Star*

Tillage, Leon Walter. *Leon's Story*

Yates, Elizabeth. *Amos Fortune: Free Man*

Velde, Vivian Vande

Tales from the Brothers Grimm and the Sisters Weird

LC 94-26341. 1995. 128p. $17.00 (ISBN 0-15-200220-0). Jane Yolen Books/Harcourt Brace and Company. 1997. 128p. $3.99 pa. (ISBN 0-440-41300-1). Dell Yearling.

Genres: Folklore, fantasy, humor, short stories

Themes: Fairy tales, fractured folktales, twisted tales, parodies, magic, love, royalty, power, trickery, point of view, greed, wishes, transformations

Reading level: Sixth grade

Interest level: Fourth through twelfth grade

Reviews:
Booklist. 93(9/10):764 January 1/15, 1997.
Bulletin of the Center for Children's Books.
    49(2):73 October 1995. (Recommended)
Horn Book. 72(2):201–2 March/April 1996.
School Library Journal. 42(1):126 January 1997.

Author Information

Growing up in New York City, Vivian Vande Velde was always making up stories. She liked taking a character from one story, a plot from another, and have her stuffed animals act out the result. Velde finds inspiration from other writings and generally bases her stories on genuine feelings. If some of her characters are awkward or unhappy with the way they look, it's because Velde sees that as reflective of real life. These characters will go on to face a challenge and take charge.

Plot Summary

Thirteen (of course!) well-known fairy tales are brought into the present by a process of fracturing and twisting. Traditions fly out the window as the story of "Goldilocks and the Three Bears" becomes "All Point Bulletin," "The Pied Piper of Hamlin" becomes "Excuses," "Rapunzel" becomes "And Now a Word from Our Sponsor," and so forth.

Introducing the Book

These wacky stories with equally odd illustrations will need little selling. The stories vary in length from half a page to twenty-six pages. Read the very short "All Points Bulletin" or "Rated PG-13" to sell the book to potential readers.

Booktalks

On the Spot

Tales from the Brothers Grimm and the Sisters Weird are fractured and twisted every witch way—pun intended! Familiar fairy tales be gone! These tales are grim and weird!

With the Author's Words

Once upon a time, in a land where even parents had magic, a mother got so upset with her son's bad temper, sloppy clothes, messy room, and disgusting table manners that she said: "If you're going to act like a beast, you might as well look like one, too." (p. 109, hardback edition)

Thus begins the story of "Beauty and the Beast." It's just one of many reversed and twisted tales told by the Brothers Grimm and the Sisters Weird!

Literature Extensions/Alternative Book Report Activities

Creative Writing/Fractured Folktales/Internet—Share the rules featured on the inside flyleaf of the *Tales from the Brothers Grimm and Sisters Weird* book jacket ("How to fracture a fairy tale: 1. Make the villain a hero. 2. Make the hero a villain. 3. Tell what really happened. 4. All of the above") . Working in groups or individually, students can fracture tales they already know.

Another creative writing activity can focus on the phrase "Once upon a time." Eight of the stories begin with a very funny "Once upon a time" sentence with a reference to today's world. For example, the Rumpelstiltzkin story "Straw into Gold" begins, "Once upon a time, in the days before Social Security or insurance companies, there lived a miller. . . ." Students can rewrite or create "Once upon a time" sentences for any fairy tale. Also look at *Prince Cinders* by Babette Cole (G. P. Putnam's Sons, 1987), which pokes fun at current issues and mores.

Drama/Readers' Theater—Many of these stories would be delightfully funny performed as either a play or as readers' theater. Consult Aaron Shepard's "Readers on Stage: Tips for Reader's Theater" at http://www.aaronshep.com/rt/ROS.html for "an online guide to scripting, staging, and performing."

Folktales/Literature/Variants—Use Velde's short Cinderella story, "Evidence," as a connection to more than 500 variants noted in the beginning of *Princess Furball* by Charlotte Huck (Greenwillow Books, 1989). Students can find other versions, such as *Yeh Shen: A Cinderella Story from China* by Ai Ling Louie (G. P. Putnam's Sons, 1982); *Egyptian Cinderella* by Shirley Climo (Harper, 1989); *The Rough-Face Girl* by Rafe Martin (G. P. Putnam's Sons, 1992); and *Cinderella* by Charles Perrault and illustrated by Susan Jeffers (Dial Books for Young Readers, 1990) for comparison. More Cinderella citations are included in the "Tales of a glass slipper" bookmark. How do these various stories represent different times and cultures?

Also provide *Ella Enchanted* by Gail Carson Levine (HarperCollins, 1997) for an absorbing novelized version featuring a spunky and endearing Cinderella who falls in love and overcomes a curse.

Literature/Folklore/Frog Prince/Transformations—Even though Prince Sidney tried to help the old woman at the well, she still changed him into a "bulgy-eyed green frog" (p. 27, hardback edition). Provide other variations of the Grimms' frog prince story, such as: *The Frog Prince, or, Iron Henry* by Jacob Grimm and Wilhelm Grimm and illustrated by Binette Schroeder (North-South Books 1989); *A Frog Prince* by Alix Berenzy (Henry Holt and Company, 1989); *The Princess and the Frog* by Rachel Isadora (Greenwillow Books, 1989); and *The Frog Prince, Continued* by Jon Scieszka (Viking, 1991).

Transformations and magical spells in folk literature are common across many cultures. Introduce this folktale element, or motif, using the following transformation examples to expand a study: The Norwegian prince transforms into a bear in "East of the Sun and West of the Moon," the French prince into a beast in "Beauty and the Beast," and the Japanese bird into a human in "The Crane Wife." Also include some of the many Native American stories featuring animal-to-human and human-to-animal transformations, such as *The Enchanted Caribou* by Elizabeth Cleaver (Atheneum, 1985); *Buffalo Woman* by Paul Gobel (Bradbury Press, 1984); and *Where the Buffaloes Begin* by Olaf Baker (Frederick Warne, 1981).

Tales of a Glass Slipper . . .

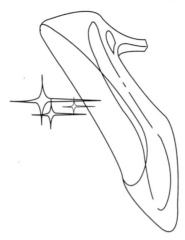

Climo, Shirley. *Egyptian Cinderella*

Coburn, Jewell Reinhart, and Tzexa Cherta Lee. *Jouanah: A Hmong Cinderella*

Hooks, William. *Moss Gown*

Huck, Charlotte. *Princess Furball*

Jacobs, Joseph. *Tattercoats*

Jeffers, Susan. *Cinderella*

Jungman, Ann. *Cinderella and the Hot Air Balloon*

Levine, Gail Garson. *Ella Enchanted*

Louie, Ai-Ling. *Yeh Shen, A Cinderella Story from China*

Martin, Rafe. *The Rough-Face Girl*

Meddaugh, Susan. *Cinderella's Rat*

Fairy Tales: The Long Version

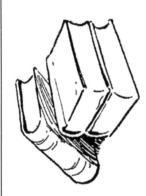

Dahl, Roald. *Dahl's Revolting Rhymes*

de Lint, Charles. *Jack the Giant Killer*

Geras, Adele. *Egerton Hall Trilogy*

Levine, Gail Garson. *Ella Enchanted*

McKinley, Robin. *Beauty: A Retelling of the Story of Beauty and the Beast*

McKinley, Robin. *Door in the Hedge*

McKinley, Robin. *Rose Daughter*

Napoli, Donna Jo. *The Magic Circle*

Napoli, Donna Jo. *Zel*

Skurzynski, Gloria. *What Happened in Hamelin*

Straus, Gwenn. *Trail of Stones*

Wrede, Patricia. *Snow White and Rose Red*

Yolen, Jane. *Briar Rose*

Short and Sassy Twisted Tales: Picture Books

Brothers Grimm. *The Frog Prince: Retold with a Twist*. Illus. by Alix Berenzy

Cole, Babette. *Princess Smartypants*

Fleischman, Paul. *Shadow Play*

French, Fiona. *Snow White in New York*

Ghilip, Neil. *Fairy Tales of the Brothers Grimm*

Jackson, Ellen B. *Cinder-Edna*

Palatini, Maggie. *Piggie Pie*

Scieszka, Jon. *The Frog Prince, Continued*

Scieszka, Jon. *The Stinky Cheese Man and Other Fairly Stupid Tales*

Scieszka, Jon. *The True Story of the Three Little Pigs*

Trivizas, Eugene. *The Three Little Wolves and the Big Bad Pig*

Tunnel, Michael O. *Beauty and the Beastly Children*

Turkle, Brinton. *Deep in the Forest*

Velde, Vivian Vande. *Tales from the Brothers Grimm and the Sisters Weird*

Vozar, David. *Yo, Hungry Wolf: A Nursery Rap*

Williams, Marcia
The Adventures of Robin Hood

LC 94-10436. 1995. unpaged. $17.95 (ISBN 1-56402-535-7). Candlewick Press. 1997. 32p. $7.99pa. (ISBN 0-763-60275-2). Candlewick Press.

Genres: Graphic novel, comics, adventure, humor, traditional literature

Themes: Robin Hood, heroes, folklore, legends, England, medieval times, Sherwood, bandits, justice, poaching, outlaws, robbers, theft, oppression, tyranny, greed, taxes, archery, acceptance, justice, poverty, kindness, orphans, British folklore, puns

Reading level: Fifth grade

Interest level: Third grade and up

Reviews:
Booklist. 91(14):1327 March 15, 1995.
Publishers Weekly. 242(5):100 January 30, 1995. (Starred review)
School Library Journal. 41(4):148 April 1995.

Author Information

Formerly a nursery school teacher, Marcia Williams has also been a papier mâché and cloth sculptor and an interior designer. She has illustrated several children's books using a comic-strip style. A London, England, resident, Williams retold and illustrated the Robin Hood legend because her son is an avid fan of Robin Hood. She feels the tale continues to be popular and relevant even today.

Plot Summary

Eleven colorful, funny, and exciting adventures of Robin Hood and his band are featured in comic-strip style. From Robin's early days as a homeless outlaw to his altercations with the greedy Prince John and wicked Sheriff of Nottingham, the stories reveal the adventures of the famous Merry Men of Sherwood Forest.

Introducing the Book

Students introduced to books in graphic novel or comic book format will need little introduction and even less encouragement to take them off your hands. Just booktalk it, display it, and watch kids read!

Booktalks

On the Spot

Come to Sherwood Forest and meet Robin Hood and his Merry Men in this comic retelling of a famous legend!

With the Author's Words

As usual, Robin and his Merry Men have been tricking and fooling the Sheriff of Nottingham and his men.

> *The prince warned the Sheriff of Nottingham that either he or Robin must go. So the sheriff [and his side kicks] hatched a plot. They announced an archery contest to be held at Nottingham. First prize was to be a golden arrow. Robin, as his enemies had hoped, could not resist the chance to prove himself the finest archer in England. ("The Golden Arrow" story, p. 15, hardback edition)*

Where's Robin? Find him on this double-page spread in *The Adventures of Robin Hood* and discover how he tricked the sheriff again!

Literature Extensions/Alternative Book Report Activities

Film Festival/Robin Hood—The legend of Robin Hood has been popular for movie producers; numerous films are available. Pull together a festival featuring a variety of these films, such as the spoof *Robin Hood: Men in Tights* (TFC/Brooksfilms, 1993); Kevin Costner's *Robin Hood: Prince of Thieves* (Warner Brothers, 1991), known for its music but not the acting; *Robin Hood* (Walt Disney Productions, 1973), with a cast of animal characters; Errol Flynn's *Robin Hood* (Warner Brothers, 1947); and *The Adventures of Robin Hood* (Warner Brothers, 1938), which won several Academy Awards.

History/Home Economics—The medieval English setting of *The Adventures of Robin Hood* provides inspiration to celebrate with a feast. Use Aliki's *A Medieval Feast* (Crowell, 1983), along with *Food & Feasts in the Middle Ages* by Imogen Dawson (New Discovery Books, 1994); *The Middle Ages* by Sarah Howarth (Viking, 1993); and *Fourteenth-Century Towns* by John D. Clare (Harcourt Brace and Company, 1993) to help with the planning. Students can wear befitting costumes and cook food that traditionally would have been served. What appropriate entertainment can students provide? Contact your local Society of Creative Anachronisms and invite them to visit your class (in full costume) with demonstrations and information about medieval times.

Sports/Archery—The Golden Arrow contest episode features archery, a sport in which Robin excelled. Because students like learning unusual sports, invite an archer to demonstrate and teach. Provide information about the National Field Archery Association, archery as an Olympic event, and so forth.

Traditional Literature/Legends/Heroes/SuperHeroes/Writing—Assemble a collection of picture books about legendary characters, such as *John Henry* by Julius Lester (Dial, 1994); *Dragons: Truth, Myth, and Legend* by David Passes (Western Publishing, 1993); *Larger Than Life: The Adventures of American Legendary Heroes* by Robert D. San Souci (Doubleday, 1991); and *The Enchanted Caribou* by Elizabeth Cleaver (Atheneum, 1985) to use with *The Adventures of Robin Hood* to launch a study about legends and heroic characters. What are the characteristics of a legendary hero? Why are they culturally important? What makes them fun to read about?

After studying heroes of the past, explore such comic superheroes as Superman and Batgirl. Who will be the heroes of the future? Students, working individually or in a group, can develop the archetype of a future hero using illustrations and stories. A helpful guide linking legendary heroes of mythology to those who are popular now is *Once Upon a Galaxy* by Josepha Sherman (August House Publishers, 1994).

Illustrated Classics

Cervantes, Miguel De. *Don Quixote.* Illus. by Marcia Williams

Grimm, Jacob, and Wilhelm Grimm. *Fairy Tales of the Brothers Grimm.* Illus. by David Wenzel

Tolkien, J. R. R. *The Hobbit: Or, There and Back Again.* Illus. by David Wenzel

Verne, Jules, et al. *A Journey to the Center of the Earth.* Illus. by Joe Boddy

Williams, Marcia. *The Adventures of Robin Hood*

Williams, Marcia. *Greek Myths for Young Children*

Williams, Marcia. *The Iliad and the Odyssey*

Williams, Marcia. *King Arthur and the Knights of the Round Table*

Medieval Reads

Furlong, Monica. *Robin's Country*

Kirwan, Anna Juliet. *A Dream Takes Off*

Platt, Richard. *Stephen Biesty's Cross-Sections: Castle*

San Souci, Robert D. *Young Merlin*

Skurzynski, Gloria. *What Happened in Hamelin*

Twain, Mark. *A Connecticut Yankee in King Arthur's Court*

Williams, Marcia. *The Adventures of Robin Hood*

Yolen, Jane. *Hobby: The Young Merlin Trilogy*

Yolen, Jane. *Merlin: The Young Merlin Trilogy*

Yolen, Jane. *Passager: The Young Merlin Trilogy*

Robin in the Hood

Early, Margaret. *Robin Hood*

Friesner, Ester. *The Sherwood Game*

Furlong, Monica. *Robin's Country*

Heyer, Carol. *Robin Hood*

McKinley, Robin. *The Outlaws of Sherwood*

Morpurgo, Michael. *Robin of Sherwood*

Philip, Neil. *Robin Hood*

Pyle, Howard. *The Merry Adventures of Robin Hood*

Sutcliff, Rosemary. *Chronicles of Robin Hood*

Tomlinson, Theresa. *The Forestwife*

Williams, Marcia. *The Adventures of Robin Hood*

More Rip-Roaring Reads
for High School Students

Burks, Brian

Runs With Horses

LC 95-8460. 1995. 118p. $11.00 (ISBN 0-152-00264-2). Harcourt Brace and Company, 1995. 118p. $5.00pa. (ISBN 0-15-200994- 9). Harcourt Brace and Company.

Genres: Historical fiction, adventure, multicultural

Themes: Apache Indians, Indians of North America, coming-of-age, traditions, Geronimo, reservations, warriors, pride, honor, hunger, survival, guns, training, war, battle, alcohol abuse, surrender, raids, courage, hunting, horses, anger, fear

Reading level: Fifth grade

Interest level: Fifth through tenth grade

Reviews:
The Book Report. 14(4):40 January/February 1996.
Booklist. 92(5):464 November 1, 1995.
Bulletin of the Center for Children's Books. 49(4):121 December 1995. (Recommended)
School Library Journal. 41(11):119 November 1995.

Author Information

A writer of classic westerns for adults, Brian Burks's interest in the Apache Indians guided his search for information on the last free group of the Chiricahua Apaches. The result was no information, so he wrote *Runs With Horses*, his first novel for young adults. Burks has had a variety of occupations—cowboy, blacksmith, ambulance driver, and range rider. He now works as a rancher, horse trainer, and professional musician when he is not writing. Tularosa, New Mexico, is home to Burks, his wife, and their five children.

Plot Summary

The year is 1886, when Runs With Horses is sixteen years old and a member of the last Chiricahua Apache band, under the leadership of Geronimo. They are on the run to avoid assimilation and reservation life and are being pursued by both the U.S. and Mexican governments. Fighting for survival, Geronimo trains the last group of Apache warriors, including Runs With Horses. He excels and can hardly wait until he becomes a man in the Apache tradition.

Introducing the Book

Read aloud to page 8 to lure reluctant readers to this compact, action-filled, fast-paced novel. The map preceding the prologue helps orient readers. The epilogue and bibliography provide sources and information for history buffs.

Booktalks

On the Spot

Runs With Horses has many difficult tasks to complete to become a warrior. He runs fast, he hunts well, he tracks silently, but can he save his people from destruction?

With the Author's Words

Runs With Horses wants to become an Apache warrior in Geronimo's band. The trials he must face are exciting and physically demanding; failure is unthinkable.

> *Runs With Horses moved beside Stands Alone, the unmarried warrior who was to accompany him. . . . A tight, apprehensive feeling grew in his stomach as the brave stooped to lift a water jug from the ground beside them. Could he do it? Could he run the three miles to the top of the mountain and then back without swallowing or spitting out the mouthful of water? (p. 5, hardback edition)*

This is one of many tests Runs With Horses must pass in order to become a man who can help his people survive.

Literature Extensions/Alternative Book Report Activities

History/American/Indian Chiefs/Internet—Geronimo, the leader of Runs With Horses's Apache band, is one of the most famous Indian chiefs. Using the following references, students can discover more about Geronimo and other powerful Indian leaders: *Indian Chiefs* (Holiday House, 1992) and *The Life and Death of Crazy Horse* (Holiday House, 1996), both by Russell Freedman; *The Great Indian Chiefs: Cochise, Geronimo, Crazy Horse, Sitting Bull* by Jean-Robert Masson (Barron's Juveniles, 1994); and the Internet site "Powerful People" at http://www.powersource.com/powersource/gallery/people/default.html.

History/Native Cultures/Western Expansion/Assimilation—Runs With Horses's Apache band struggled to avoid assimilation and reservation life imposed on Native Americans during the period of western expansion. Forced to move to reservations, many Indians rightfully feared their cultures would be lost. Students can study further about this difficult period in U.S. history by consulting the following books: *A Strange and Distant Shore: Indians of the Great Plains in Exile* by Brent Ashabranner (Cobblehill, 1996); *Native Americans and the Reservation in American History* by Anita Louise McCormick (Enslow, 1996); *White Bead Ceremony* by Sherrin Watkins (Council Oak Publishing, 1994); and *In a Sacred Manner I Live: Native American Wisdom,* edited by Neil Philip (Clarion Books, 1997).

Some students or classes may want to focus on other native cultures whose lands were encroached upon, such as the Canadian First Nation people and the Australian Aborigines. See *This Land Is My Land* by George Littlechild (Children's Book Press, 1993) for a Canadian perspective.

Sociology/Cultural Anthropology/Rites of Passage/Research—Runs With Horses is going through his Apache tribe's rite of passage in order to become a warrior. For Apache girls, a coming-of-age ceremony is celebrated through special dances and prayers as described in *The Gift of Changing Woman* by Tryntje Van Ness Seymour (Henry Holt and Company, 1993). Different cultures and different times proscribe rites of passage for adolescents. What coming-of-age events and activities do today's teenagers experience? Some of these may include obtaining a driver's license, body piercing, and tattoos. Interested students can research the concept of "rites of passage" further on the Internet, through periodical indexes, and through interviews with sociologists or cultural anthropologists.

Sociology/Guns—A gun in Runs With Horses's band was a symbol of manhood and success. Replacing his father's lost gun was very important to Runs With Horses. Provide stories that focus on guns in other settings, including *The Rifle* by Gary Paulsen (Harcourt Brace and Company, 1995); *Twelve Shots: Outstanding Short Stories About Guns,* edited by Harry Mazer (Delacorte Press, 1997); and the picture book *Just One Flick of a Finger,* written by Marybeth Lorbiecki and illustrated by David Diaz (Dial Books for Young Readers, 1996).

Initiate a study of guns and their effect on humankind throughout history—both the negative and the positive aspects. Student research can focus on the development of firearms, the role of guns in western expansion, the role of the National Rifle Association in policy making, guns and violence, gun control laws, and so on.

Living in Two Worlds: Native American Kids

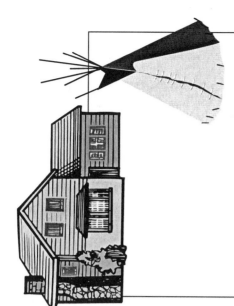

Ashabranner, Brent. *To Live in Two Worlds: American Indian Youth Today*

Driving Hawk Sneve, Virginia. *Dancing Teepees: Poems of American Youth*

Hirschfelder, Arlene B., and Beverly R. Singer. *Rising Voices: Writings of Young Native Americans*

Hobbs, Will. *Bearstone*

Keegan, Marcia. *Pueblo Boy: Growing Up in Two Worlds*

Lipsyte, Robert. *The Brave*

Lipsyte, Robert. *The Chief*

Lipsyte, Robert. *The Contender*

Seymour, Tryntje Van Ness. *The Gift of Changing Woman*

The Past— Indian Teens

Blevins, Win. *Stone Song*

Burks, Brian. *Runs With Horses*

Dorris, Michael. *Sees Behind Trees*

Gregory, Kristiana. *Jenny of the Tetons*

Hudson, Jan. *Dawn Rider*

Hudson, Jan. *Sweetgrass*

McKissack, Patricia C. *Run Away Home*

Meyers, Carolyn. *Where the Broken Heart Still Beats*

O'Dell, Scott. *Sing Down the Moon*

O'Dell, Scott, and Elizabeth Hall. *Thunder Rolling in the Mountains*

Quick Reads About Our Past

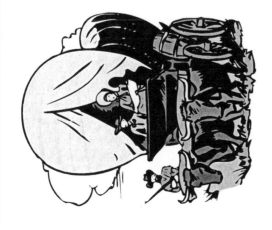

Burks, Brian. *Runs With Horses*

DeFelice, Cynthia. *Weasel*

Dorris, Michael. *Morning Girl*

Fleischman, Paul. *The Borning Room*

Fleischman, Paul. *Bull Run*

Fleischman, Paul. *Saturnalia*

Paulsen, Gary. *Nightjohn*

Paulsen, Gary. *Sarny: A Life Remembered*

Robinet, Harriette Gillem. *If You Please, President Lincoln*

Stolz, Mary. *Cezanne Pinto*

Cooney, Caroline B.

Flash Fire

LC 94-43805. 1995. 198p. $14.95 (ISBN 0-590-25253-4).
Scholastic. 1996. $4.50pa. (ISBN 0-590-48496-6pa.).
Scholastic.

Genres: Contemporary realistic fiction, adventure

Themes: Natural disasters, disasters, wildfires, survival, fire fighting, cooperation, brothers and sisters, danger, emotional neglect, selfishness, independence, neighbors, friendship, love, parents, looters, panic, death

Reading level: Fifth grade

Interest level: Sixth through twelfth grade

Reviews:
> *The Book Report.* 14(4):41 January/February 1996.
> *Booklist.* 92(5):464 November 1, 1995.
> *Bulletin of the Center for Children's Books.* 49(5):157 January 1996. (Recommended)
> *School Library Journal.* 41(2):128 December 1995.
> *Voice of Youth Advocates.* 18(5):298 December 1995. (#4 quality, #5 popularity)

Author Information

Caroline B. Cooney was born and raised in Connecticut and still lives there in a small town. She began writing mysteries in college because those were the books she preferred to read. Since she was first published at age 30, Cooney has written more than 100 books for children and young adults. Cooney has two daughters (who are avid readers) and one son (who has helped her understand reluctant readers). She tried four colleges but feels her real education has come from reading seemingly millions of books.

Plot Summary

This minute-by-minute account of a Los Angeles wildfire spans one hour and forty minutes. No one suspected the wealthy, well-kept homes in narrow Pinch Canyon would be in danger, especially the parents of those kids left at home on their own. The fire is terrifying and unpredictable, and the children have to save themselves.

Introducing the Book

The minute-by-minute notations focus the reader's attention on the immediacy of this book. The story is riveting and difficult to put down once it's started. With the rise of the Santa Ana winds and the arrival of the California fire season in the fall, consider reading aloud to the end of "the brushfire 3:21 P.M." section on page 15 (paperback edition).

Booktalks

On the Spot

The fires burning in nearby Los Angeles have been the exciting news story on TV for days. But that has not affected Danna; her life is still incredibly boring. What Danna doesn't know is that in about 45 minutes a *Flash Fire* will sweep down her canyon . . . totally out of control.

With the Author's Words

Firefighter

> Matt Marsh was the happiest, most excited twenty-two-year-old in the great state of California. It was the big game. And he was on the team. He was wearing a new helmet, since the old one had melted fighting yesterday's Altadena fire, and he was using, of course, a new hose, since the one he had held to save his own life had also melted. Matt referred to the fires in sport terms: The score, for example was: 100,000 acres burned, 240 houses destroyed, 44 casualties, no deaths. In some weird way, Matt was cheering for the fire. He was awed by it. Stunned by it. Fascinated by it. They were fighting it hard and relentlessly, and yet it was winning. (p. 27, paperback edition)

Already the fire is winning, and it hasn't even reached Danna and Hall's home in Pinch Canyon.

Literature Extensions/Alternative Book Report Activities

Current Events/Video—Danna owns a home video camera and thinks the encroaching fire is good material. "You and I are going to get great footage. Where is that camera?" (p. 89, paperback edition). In the last few years, television viewers have noticed more and more news segments shot by amateur videographers. Weather phenomena, crimes, disasters, and accidents are all fodder for the ubiquitous camcorder. Students interested in perfecting their videotaping ability can receive professional training at little or no cost if your community has a public or community television access center. Contact the Alliance for Community Media by telephone at (202) 393-2650 or by e-mail at acm@alliancecm.org to see if such a station exists in your community.

Current Events/Wildfires/Internet—In California, the most destructive wildfires typically occur in September, October, and early November when the Santa Ana winds blow and the moisture is scarce. Introduce a study of this current event by reading aloud Patricia Polacco's picture book *Tikvah Means Hope* (Doubleday, 1994).

However, all wildfires are not limited to California. In recent years, many states, such as Oregon, Florida, Michigan, and Pennsylvania, have had their share. The United States Forest Service's "Wildland Fire Assessment System" Website at http://www.fs.fed.us/land/wfas/welcome.html keeps track of fire weather and fire danger. Students can access daily forecasts, observations, updates, maps, and archives. Other sites of interest include "Wildfires: Are You Prepared?" at http://www.ystone.mt.gov/DES/wildfire.htm and "Fire and the Forest" at http://www.umn.edu/bellmuse/firelink.html.

Sociology/Behavior/Looters/Discussion—The Swann family uses the wild fires and resulting chaos as an opportunity to steal things from the fire victims. Eve Bunting's picture book for older readers, *Smoky Night* (Harcourt Brace and Company, 1994), highlights the looting and rioting of the 1992 Los Angeles riots. Use these two accounts to serve as a basis for attention to this issue. Students may also know about rioting and looting incidents that have taken place in cities after their professional sports teams have won national championships and in countries struggling with changing political climates. A broad study can focus on a number of topics, such as economic and racial problems identified as underlying factors, crowd behavior, the psychology of looting, the economic burden to business owners, emergency action, restoring the peace, and improving conditions for the future.

Parenting/Life Skills—The parents featured in *Flash Fire* are certainly not model caregivers. After reading the book, students can compare and contrast the parenting skills (or lack of them) as seen in the three families. Students can subsequently look for positive parenting alternatives mentioned in such books as *Are We Having Fun Yet? The 16 Secrets of Happy Parenting* by Kay Willis and Maryann Bucknum Brinley (Warner Books, 1997); *The Parent's Journal Guide to Raising Great Kids* by Bobbi Conner (Bantam Books, 1997); *Common Sense Parenting: A Proven, Step-by-Step Guide for Raising Responsible Kids and Building Happy Families* by Raymond V. Burke (Boys Town Press, 1996); and *Time-Out for Children* by Barbara Albers Hill (Avery Publishers, 1997).

Fire Fighting— The Real Story

Cone, Patrick. *Wildfire*

Greenberg, Keith Elliot. *Smokejumper: Firefighter from the Sky*

Jenkins, Starr. *Smokejumpers, '49: Brothers in the Sky*

Maclean, Norman. *Young Men & Fire*

Pyne, Stephen J. *Fire on the Rim: A Firefighter's Season at the Grand Canyon*

Smith, Dennis. *Firefighters: Their Lives in Their Own Words*

Stewart, Gail. *Smokejumpers & Forest Firefighters*

Disasters!
Natural and Man-Made

Carson, Jo. *The Great Shaking: An Account of the Earthquakes of 1811 and 1812 by a Bear Who Was a Witness, New Madrid, Missouri*

Cooney, Caroline. *Flash Fire*

Cytron, Barry D. *Fire! The Library Is Burning*

Gregory, Kristiana. *Earthquake at Dawn*

Hesse, Karen. *Phoenix Rising*

Kehret, Peg. *Earthquake Terror*

Murphy, Jim. *The Great Fire*

Nance, John J. *Pandora's Clock*

Pausewang, Gudrun. *Fall-Out*

Peck, Richard. *Ghosts I Have Been*

Ure, Jean. *Plague*

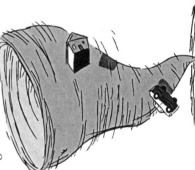

Can't Put It Down! Caroline Cooney Wrote It!

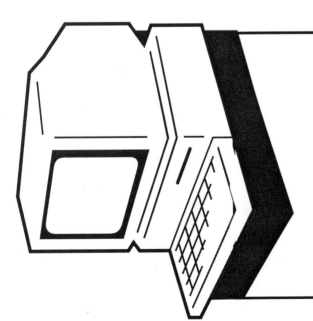

Both Sides of Time

Don't Blame the Music

Driver's Ed

Emergency Room

The Face on the Milk Carton

Flash Fire

Flight #116 Is Down

I'm Not Your Other Half

Out of Time

Terrorist

Twenty Pageants Later

The Voice on the Radio

Whatever Happened to Janie?

Cushman, Karen
Catherine, Called Birdy

LC 93-23333. 1994. 170p. $14.95 (ISBN 0-395-68186-3). Clarion Books. 1995. 212p. $3.95pa. (ISBN 0-06-440584-2). HarperTrophy. Abridged audiocassette. 1996. $16.99 (ISBN 0-553-47669-6). Bantam Books-Audio. 5 cassettes/6.5 hours. 1997. $42.00 (ISBN 0-7887-0687-X). Recorded Books.

Genre: Historical fiction

Themes: Medieval life, Middle Ages, England, diaries, independence, gender roles, women, marriage, hope, determination, folk medicine, saints, religion, friendship, cleverness, Crusades, birds, reading, writing, love, jealousy

Reading level: Seventh grade

Interest level: Seventh through twelfth grade

Reviews:

The Book Report. 13(4):46 January/February 1995.

Booklist. 90(16):1526 April 15, 1994.

Bulletin of the Center for Children's Books. 47(10):316 June 1994. (Recommended)

Horn Book. 70(4):457–58 July/August 1994.

Kliatt Paperback and Audio Book Guide. 29(5):8 September 1995.

Publishers Weekly. 243(35):46 August 26, 1996.

School Library Journal. 40(6):147 June 1994. (Starred review)

Voice of Youth Advocates. 17(2):81 June 1994. (#4 quality, #4 popularity)

Author Information

Karen Cushman, an assistant director of the Museum Studies Department at John F. Kennedy University in San Francisco, has been interested in history for years. She had access to countless resources about medieval times, including thirteenth-century etiquette, such as "Don't blow your nose in the tablecloth." Cushman was curious about "ordinary young people in other times" instead of the usual knights and royalty. This inspired the writing of *Catherine, Called Birdy*, which took her three years to finish and was accepted by her publisher almost immediately.

Plot Summary

Young teenager Catherine, nicknamed Birdy (she keeps birds as pets), is the daughter of an English knight living in the thirteenth century. She is determined not to be married off against her will, and challenges her father ("the Beast") about his potential husbands for her and everything else. Recording her thoughts and escapades in a diary, Catherine reveals an unromantic and authentic look at the "upstairs and downstairs" of medieval life from the point of view of a spunky, intelligent young woman.

Introducing the Book

The thirteen-chapter diary is divided by months (September to September). The five-page author's note about medieval England and a bibliography are musts for teachers. Because of the diary format and subsequent lack of dialogue, *Catherine, Called Birdy* is a more difficult read than it appears. Consider introducing the book to potential readers by sharing the first chapter aloud because it sets the scene perfectly and introduces readers to the inimitable Birdy. Access the helpful Internet resource for this book at "Carol Hurst's Children's Literature" Web site at http://www.carolhurst.com/titles/catherinecalledbirdy.html.

Booktalks

On the Spot

Catherine's father wants her to marry the disgusting Shaggy Beard. Catherine is resourceful and stubborn, but her father is in charge. Will she become Lady Shaggy Beard? She reveals all in her diary.

With the Author's Words

(Prop: Use parchment-type paper to write the following entry in calligraphy to make a facsimile of a page from Catherine's diary.)

The year is 1290. The place is medieval England. The writer is thirteen-year-old Catherine.

19ᵀᴴ DAY OF SEPTEMBER

I am delivered! My mother and I have made a bargain. I may forgo spinning as long as I write this account for Edward. My mother is not much for writing but has it in her heart to please Edward, especially now he is gone to be a monk, and I would do worse things to escape the foolish boredom of spinning. So I will write. What follows will be my book—the book of Catherine, called Little Bird or Birdy. . . . The writing I learned of my brother Edward, but the words are my own.

Picked off twenty-nine fleas today. (p. 2, hardback and paperback editions)

Literature Extensions/Alternative Book Report Activities

Art/Calligraphy—Every chapter in *Catherine, Called Birdy* begins with an illuminated letter. (Note: The calligraphy styles differ in the paperback and hardback editions.) Birdy is fortunate because she knows how to read and write; she was taught by her brother, Edward, a monk whose life work is creating illuminations. Inspire students to experiment with calligraphy by sharing the following books: *Illuminations* by Jonathan Hunt (Bradbury, 1989); *Bibles and Bestiaries: A Guide to Illuminated Manuscripts* by Elizabeth B. Wilson (Farrar, Straus & Giroux, 1994); and *Book* by Karen Brookfield (Alfred A. Knopf, 1993). Whereas beginning calligraphy students generally use an italic script, more advanced students will enjoy learning more challenging scripts as illustrated in the books above. Invite a calligrapher to demonstrate and teach the techniques necessary.

History/Middle Ages—*Catherine, Called Birdy* gives readers an accurate, unromantic picture of medieval life, including detailed information about food, feast days, manners, manors, tenant farmers, arranged marriages, attitudes toward Jews, the harvest, fairs, Saints' Days, superstitions, public hangings, mummers, games, seasonal life, folk medicine, and so forth. This provides a natural springboard for a complete study (and perhaps schoolwide celebration) of the Middle Ages.

The following books (including excellent picture books) will provide additional information along with details about clothing, recipes, customs, and the like: Aliki's *A Medieval Feast* (Crowell, 1983); *Food & Feasts in the Middle Ages* by Imogen Dawson (New Discovery Books, 1994); *Fabulous Feasts: Medieval Cookery and Ceremony* by Madeleine Pelner Cosman (Braziller, 1976); *Fast and Feast: Food in Medieval Society* by Bridget Ann Henisch (Pennsylvania State University Press, 1976); *The Oxford Illustrated History of Medieval Europe,* edited by George Holmes (Oxford University Press, 1988); *The Middle Ages* by Sarah Howarth (Viking, 1993); *Anno's Medieval World* by Mitsumasa Anno (Philomel Books, 1979); *Fourteenth-Century Towns* by John D. Clare (Harcourt Brace and Company, 1993); and *The Luttrell Village: Country Life in the Middle Ages* by Sheila Sancha (Crowell, 1982). Also invite local members of the Society of Creative Anachronisms to stage reenactments of Middle Age tournaments, dress in period garb, and share their knowledge and passion for and about this historical period.

History/Women's Roles/Internet—The woman's role in medieval England was one of "dignity, and duty and obedience," and "girls were mostly trained for marriage. Marriage among the noble classes was not a matter of love but economics." (pp. 167–68, hardback edition; pp. 210–11, paperback edition) Birdy describes "lady-lessons" in the "8th Day of May" entry. Using this information, students can research the plight of women in this period and compare their lives to women's roles in other societies and cultures, both in the past and present. An appropriate time to focus this study would be in March during Women's History Month. Visit an Internet site about "Woman's History" at http://www.feminist.org/other/wh_menu.html.

Science/Folk Medicine—As a daughter of the manor, Catherine is frequently called upon to provide remedies and healing for a variety of ailments, such as eye infections, hangovers, sore throats, flatulence, childbirth, and liver pain. She uses such natural ingredients as wormwood, mint, cobwebs, mustard seed, snakes, sow bugs, moss, goose grease, peony root, and the like. Modern-day herbalists use some of these same ingredients, and student research can point to remedies that are still in use.

Make the following reference books available for further information: *Folklore on the American Land* by Duncan Emrich (Little, Brown and Company, 1972); *Rodale's Illustrated Encyclopedia of Herbs* by Claire Kowalchik and William H. Hylton (Rodale, 1987); *Earth Care Annual* (Rodale, 1990–); *Simon & Schuster's Guide to Plants and Flowers* by Francesco Bianchini and Azzurra Carrasa Pantano (Simon & Schuster, 1989); *Folk Medicine* by Marc Kusinitz (Chelsea House, 1991); and *Chinese Herbal Medicine* by Daniel P. Reid (Shambhala Publications, 1992).

Diaries

Anonymous. *Go Ask Alice*

Bell, William. *Forbidden City: A Novel of Modern China*

Blos, Joan W. *A Gathering of Days*

Cushman, Karen. *Catherine, Called Birdy*

Diary Project
http://www.well.com/user/diary

DiPerna, Paula. *The Discoveries of Mrs. Christopher Columbus: Wife's Version*

Filipovic, Zlata. *Zlata's Diary: A Child's Life in Sarajevo*

Frank, Anne. *The Diary of a Young Girl*

Hamilton, Morse. *Effie's House*

Hesse, Karen. *Letters from Rifka*

Pfeffer, Susan Beth. *The Year Without Michael*

Rinaldi, Ann. *Wolf by the Ears*

Schami, Rafik. *A Hand Full of Stars*

Capable Girls

Alexander, Lloyd. *Vesper Holly* series

Ashby, Ruth, and Deborah Gore Ohrn. *Herstory: Women Who Changed the World*

Avi. *The True Confessions of Charlotte Doyle*

Colman, Penny. *Rosie the Riveter: Women Working on the Home Front in World War II*

Cushman, Karen. *Catherine, Called Birdy*

Dickinson, Peter. *A Bone from a Dry Sea*

Johnson, Angela. *Toning the Sweep*

Keller, Helen. *Helen Keller: The Story of My Life*

Kramer, Barbara. *Alice Walker*

O'Dell, Scott. *Carlota*

Ponce, Mary Helen. *Taking Control*

Pullman, Philip. *The Golden Compass*

Staples, Suzanne Fisher. *Shabanu*

Temple, Frances. *Tonight, by Sea*

Medieval Times

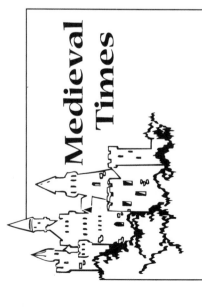

Amoss, Berthe. *Lost Magic*

Bradford, Karleen. *There Will Be Wolves*

Cushman, Karen. *Catherine, Called Birdy*

Cushman, Karen. *The Midwife's Apprentice*

Garden, Nancy. *Dove and Sword: A Novel of Joan of Arc*

Kirwan, Anna. *Juliet: A Dream Takes Flight, England, 1339*

Konigsburg, E. L. *A Proud Taste of Scarlet and Miniver*

McKinley, Robin. *The Outlaws of Sherwood*

Pope, Elisabeth. *The Perilous Gard*

Sutcliff, Rosemary. *The Witch's Brat*

Temple, Frances. *The Ramsay Scallop*

Tomlinson, Theresa. *The Forestwife*

Eisner, Will

Dropsie Avenue:
The Neighborhood

LC 95-13159. 1995. 170p. $15.95
(ISBN 0-87816-348-4). Kitchen Sink Press.

Genres: Graphic novel, comics, historical fiction, contemporary realistic fiction, multicultural

Themes: South Bronx (New York), neighborhoods, city life, family life, immigrants, ethnicity, racial conflicts, real estate, evolution, change, generations, friendship, memories, roots, stereotypes, decline, cartoons, property, politics, war brides, corruption, tenements, prohibition, bootlegging, government programs, intermarriage, gangs, spousal abuse, drug dealers, rent control, welfare, public housing, pollution

Reading level: Fourth grade

Interest level: Ninth grade and up

Reviews:
  Publishers Weekly. 242(19):293 May 8, 1995.

Author Information

Soon after Will Eisner graduated from high school in 1937, he sold his first comic feature to a magazine called *WOW.* Even though the magazine soon folded, Eisner was primed to continue writing stories in the "language of comic strips." Credited with being the creator of the graphic novel (book-length stories illustrated with comics) with the publication of *A Contract with God* (Kitchen Sink Press, 1985), Eisner founded magazines and publishing companies to produce all varieties of comics or, as he calls it, "sequential art." A longtime believer in using comics to attract reluctant readers, Eisner feels they are the perfect media for learning and teaching. The setting for *Dropsie Avenue*, a South Bronx neighborhood, is similar to Eisner's own childhood neighborhood.

Plot Summary

The rise, fall, and rebirth of a South Bronx neighborhood from the 1870s through the 1990s is featured in this graphic narrative. The author/illustrator chose a single character in each period of immigration, tracing a life through time.

Introducing the Book

Many students will be attracted to the visual appeal of this graphic novel. They may be surprised by the seriousness of the subject, but interest will be maintained by the artwork and fast-moving story.

Booktalks

On the Spot

One hundred years of living, fighting, loving, and dying . . . all on *Dropsie Avenue.*

With the Author's Words

Dropsie Avenue began to form in 1870 with a few Dutch families. One hundred years later . . .

> *eight buildings were burned to the ground. In that part of the borough over 10,000 fires were reported during the year. Hundreds of small businesses and retail shops left the area and over 17,000 jobs disappeared. Crime increased. 15,000 buildings became vacant in the surrounding neighborhood and over 60,000 people moved out of the area. Now Dropsie Avenue was "bombed out." Only one building remained standing. (pp. 154–55)*

The story of the rise and the fall of the neighborhood called *Dropsie Avenue* took place in those 100 years. It's a neighborhood that began with a single building—will it end that way, too?

Literature Extensions/Alternative Book Report Activities

Art/Creative Writing—With Eisner's work as an example, encourage students to produce their own graphic story. Working in groups or individually, students can select a topic related to current study (or select a neighborhood in their town) and develop a comic novel. Provide inspirational and how-to books, such as *The Art of Making Comic Books* by Michael Morgan Pellowski (Lerner Publications, 1995); *Guide to Cartooning* by Al Bohl (Pelican, 1997); and *Understanding Comics: The Invisible Art* by Scott McCloud (Kitchen Sink Press, 1994).

Art/Neighborhoods/Community Service Projects—In addition to *Dropsie Avenue*, many other books visually depict changing neighborhoods. John S. Goodall incorporates the use of alternating full and half pages in *The Story of an English Village* (Atheneum, 1978) and *The Story of a Main Street* (Atheneum, 1987), whereas *New Providence: A Changing Cityscape* by Renata Von Tscharner and Ronald Lee Fleming (Harcourt Brace Jovanovich, 1987) features the evolution of a mythical city during the twentieth century, and Aminah Brenda Lynn Robinson's accordion-flap book *A Street Called Home* (Harcourt Brace and Company, 1997) looks at Mount Vernon Avenue in Columbus, Ohio, in the 1940s.

Using these books as models, students can research and illustrate a neighborhood in their community. The results can be displayed in the public library, Chamber of Commerce, or local bank.

History/Immigration/Ethnicity—This graphic novel presents students with factual information concerning the different ethnic groups who settled in the Bronx from the 1870s to 1990. Have students select one of the ethnic groups represented for further research: Dutch, English, Irish, German, Italian, Jew, Spanish, African American, Gypsy, or Hassidic Jew.

Working individually or in small groups, students can discover general information about each wave of immigrants. When did they come to the United States? Why? What kind of jobs were they able to get? What contributions did they make to society?

History/Timeline—Eisner provides a decade-by-decade list of U.S. history as he traces the rise, fall, and rebirth of Dropsie Avenue. Many significant incidents are detailed. To gain a historical perspective of these key events, students can list all the historical events mentioned within the story and create an appropriate timeline. Enhance the timeline by including sketches and illustrations along with in-depth research.

That Old Gang of Mine

Cofer, Judith Ortiz. *An Island Like You: Stories of the Barrio*

Eisner, Will. *Dropsie Avenue: The Neighborhood*

Garland, Sherry. *Shadow of the Dragon*

Hinojosa, Maria. *Crews: Gang Members Talk to Maria Hinojosa*

Hinton, S. E. *The Outsiders*

Mowry, Jess. *Babylon Boyz*

Myers, Walter Dean. *Scorpions*

Nelson, Theresa. *The Beggar's Ride*

Salisbury, Graham. *Shark Bait*

Neighborhoods

Bartone, Elisa. *Peppe the Lamplighter*

Davis, Jenny. *Checking on the Moon*

Eisner, Will. *Dropsie Avenue: The Neighborhood*

Fleischman, Paul. *Seedfolks*

Goodall, John S. *The Story of a Main Street*

Goodall, John S. *The Story of an English Village*

McDonald, Megan. *The Potato Man*

Merriam, Eve. *The Inner City Mother Goose.* Illus. by David Diaz

Mowry, Jess. *Babylon Boyz*

Robinson, Aminah Brenda Lynn. *A Street Called Home*

Soto, Gary. *Neighborhood Odes*

Von Tscharner, Renata, and Ronald Lee Fleming. *New Providence: A Changing Cityscape*

Graphic Novel—

A longer and more sophisticated version of a comic book. These self-contained short stories or novellas use text and artwork to advance the plot and set new visual standards.

Bradbury, Ray. *The Ray Bradbury Chronicles* (6 volumes)

Cruse, Howard. *Stuck Rubber Baby*

Dardess, George. *Foreign Exchange: A Novel*

Eisner, Will. *The Building*

Eisner, Will. *Dropsie Avenue: The Neighborhood*

Hirsch, Karen D., ed. *Mind Riot: Coming of Age in Comix*

Pratt, George. *Enemy Ace*

Reiber, John Ney, et al. *The Books of Magic: Bindings*

Russell, P. Craig. *Fairy Tales of Oscar Wilde: The Young King and Remarkable Rocket*

Spiegleman, Art. *Maus*

Spiegleman, Art. *Maus II*

Talbot, Bryan. *The Tale of One Bad Rat*

Williams, Marcia, reteller. *The Iliad and the Odyssey*

Fleischman, Paul
Seedfolks

LC 96-26696. 1997. 80p. $13.95 (ISBN 0-06-027471-9). HarperCollins/Cotler.

Genres: Contemporary realistic fiction, multicultural

Themes: Gardens, neighborhoods, cities, points of view, monologues, communities, strangers, prejudices, friendship, cooperation, unity, productivity, renewal, diversity, mourning, immigration, homelessness, teen parents

Reading level: Fifth grade

Interest level: Fourth through twelfth grade

Reviews:
Booklist. 93(18):1573 May 15, 1997. (Starred review)
Bulletin of the Center for Children's Books. 50(11):393 July/August 1997.
Horn Book. 63(3):320 May/June 1997.
Publishers Weekly. 244(14):93 April 7, 1997.
School Library Journal. 43(5):132 May 1997. (Starred review)
Voice of Youth Advocates. 20(2):109 June 1997. (#4 quality, #4 popularity)

Author Information

Although Paul Fleischman's father is the well-known author Sid Fleischman, Paul never thought he would grow up to be a writer. Interested in shortwave radios, printing presses, history, and music, Paul Fleischman eventually discovered that he, too, was good at writing books, and his subsequent awards and honors provide proof.

The idea for *Seedfolks* came from an article in a New Age newspaper Fleischman read while eating lunch in a San Francisco bagel bakery. The article was about a psychotherapist who prescribed gardening as therapy and noted that in ancient Egypt, doctors thought the insane could be cured by walking through gardens. "That's the line that set the hook, deep," said Fleischman. It brought back memories of a therapeutic garden at a Los Angeles Veteran's hospital, a homeless garden project in Santa Cruz, and a community garden in Boston.

Plot Summary

A vacant, garbage-strewn lot in an inner-city Cleveland neighborhood becomes a thriving community garden. The story is told by thirteen characters who cultivate and grow more than vegetables; they harvest a sense of community.

Introducing the Book

It would be a shame to read this slim book aloud because it could be such a successful reading adventure for some reluctant readers. However, tempt potential readers by reading the entries from the first two characters, Kim and Ana, ending on page 8 in the hardback edition.

Booktalks

On the Spot

Sometimes folks can be isolated and wary in an inner-city neighborhood. But a few seeds, some work with the soil, and a little bit of hope can transform a vacant lot and a neighborhood of diverse people into *Seedfolks*.

With the Author's Words

Looking out her apartment window, Ana sees . . .

something strange. Down in the lot, a little black-haired girl, hiding behind that refrigerator. She was working at the dirt and looking around suspiciously all the time. Then I realized. She was burying something . . . I thought of calling up the police. Then I saw her there the next morning, and I decided I'd solve this case myself. (p. 6, hardback edition)

This little, black-haired girl is planting the first of many seeds. The crop is a neighborhood of *Seedfolks*.

Literature Extensions/Alternative Book Report Activities

Creative Writing—The thirteen characters in *Seedfolks* each have their own chapters, but dozens of other individuals are mentioned, and parts of their stories are also told. Students can select one of these other characters and write about the garden using their point of view. How do they interact with the other gardeners, and how do they change as a result? Students can also continue the stories of the original thirteen characters. What would happen to them next?

Drama/Literature/Readers' Theater—*Seedfolks* is perfect for readers' theater, and Fleischman has his own opinions about staging a successful readers' theater production. In a discussion on the Cooperative Children's Book Center (CCBC) listserv, Fleischman suggests that *Seedfolks* and his book *Bull Run* (HarperCollins, 1993) offer an opportunity to involve readers' theater participants in reading and listening if, instead of every reader having a script, the books themselves are passed "from speaker to speaker, keeping the listeners in the dark." He notes that "one of the problems with readers' theater (when performed cold) is that those who aren't speaking are reading ahead or silently reading the lines being spoken. That foreknowledge undercuts their attention to the speakers; they're not an audience, waiting to hear what happens next."

Use this technique with thirteen readers, one reader for each character. However, let each character pre-read their section to ease any anxiety and familiarize themselves with text. The character portraits at the beginning of each chapter can be enlarged or reproduced and used for simple masks. With practice, this could become a drama production for other audiences.

Activism/Community Gardens/Community Projects/Internet—*Seedfolks* was inspired in part by community garden projects with which Fleischman was familiar in Boston and Santa Cruz. Common vision and labor often create a sense of community and result in meaningful projects that satisfy real need. Conduct a search on the Internet using a multiple search engine and directory such as Internet Sleuth, http://www.isleuth.com/, searching with such keywords as "community garden." The results will give students access to discussions, Websites, maps, and other information about community gardens throughout the United States.

Students can investigate other examples of neighborhood projects and participate themselves in community-based activities. These can include Habitat for Humanity, urban murals, environmental projects, inner-city parks, public art, and so forth.

Food/Cooking/Popular Culture—In *Seedfolks*, many of the gardeners planted foods that were culturally familiar to them. Students can investigate various foods and ethnic connections. Feature an "Ethnic Fast Foods Feast" with a variety of foods, such as Mexican tacos, Native American fried bread, Chinese egg rolls or dim sum, Japanese "California" rolls, Greek gyros, Italian pizza, and the like. Be sure to include foods representing the ethnic groups from your geographic area.

Quilted Landscape: Immigrants

Bernardo, Anilu. *Fitting In*

Cofer, Judith Ortiz. *An Island Like You: Stories of the Barrio*

Cummings, Betty Sue. *Now, Ameriky*

Mohn, Nicholasa. *The Magic Shell*

Plummer, Louise. *The Romantic Obsessions and Humiliations of Annie Sehlmeier*

Pomeranc, Marion Hess. *The American Wei*

Roseman, Kenneth. *The Melting Pot: An Adventure in New York*

Shiefman, Vicky. *Good-bye to the Trees*

Strom, Yale. *Quilted Landscape: Conversations with Young Immigrants*

City Green—Growing More Than Food

Disalvo-Ryan, Dyanne. *City Green*

Hillier, Malcolm. *The Book of Container Gardening*

Hynes, H. Patricia. *A Patch of Eden; America's Inner-City Gardeners*

Joyce, David. *The Complete Container Garden*

Landman, Ruth H. *Creating Community in the City: Cooperatives and Community Gardens in Washington, D.C.*

Phillips, Sue. *A Creative, Step-by-Step Guide to Container Gardening*

Pierce, Donna. *The City Gardener's Cookbook*

Tamar, Erika. *The Garden of Happiness*

Tarling, Thomasina. *The Container Garden: A Practical Guide to Planning and Planting*

Who's Talking? Take a Look!

Avi. *Nothing but the Truth*

Fleischman, Paul. *Bull Run*

Fleischman, Paul. *Ghosts' Grace: A Poem for Four Voices*

Fleischman, Paul. *I Am Phoenix: Poems for Two Voices*

Fleischman, Paul. *Joyful Noise: Poems for Two Voices*

Fleischman, Paul. *Seedfolks*

Glenn, Mel. *Jump Ball: A Basketball Season in Poems*

Glenn, Mel. *The Taking of Room 114: A Hostage Drama in Poems*

Glenn, Mel. *Who Killed Mr. Chippendale? A Mystery in Poems*

Goble, Paul. *Iktomi and the Ducks: A Plains Indian Story*

Macaulay, David. *Black and White*

McKissack, Patricia, and Frederick McKissack. *Christmas in the Big House, Christmas in the Quarters*

Scieszka, Jon. *The Stinky Cheese Man and Other Fairly Stupid Tales*

Glenn, Mel

Who Killed Mr. Chippendale? A Mystery in Poems

LC 95-52600. 1996. 112p. $14.99 (ISBN 0-525-67530-2). Dutton/Lodestar.

Genres: Contemporary realistic fiction, poetry, mystery, multi-cultural

Themes: Murder, teachers, students, high schools, violence, snipers, school life, teacher-student relationships, society, death, immigrants, racism

Reading level: Sixth grade

Interest level: Seventh through twelfth grade

Reviews:
Booklist. 92(19):1688 June 1/15, 1996.
Bulletin of the Center for Children's Books. 49(11):372 July/August 1996.
Publishers Weekly. 243(28):85 July 8, 1996.
School Library Journal. 42(7):104 July 1996. (Starred review)
Voice of Youth Advocates. 19(5):287 December 1996. (#2 quality, #2 popularity)

Author Information

Mel Glenn grew up in Brooklyn and thought he would be a journalist after writing columns and feature stories for the undergraduate newspaper at New York University. However, following the assassination of President Kennedy, Glenn joined the Peace Corps and became an English teacher in Sierra Leone, West Africa. He discovered that he loved teaching and his students. *Who Killed Mr. Chippendale?* combines Glenn's love of writing, teaching, and his obvious understanding of students and the educational system.

Plot Summary

Reactions to a high school teacher's murder from students, colleagues, and others are presented in first-person narrative poems. In addition to the murderer's identity, readers come to know students and teachers—their strengths, weaknesses, and secrets.

Introducing the Book

The free-verse form (which many readers will not even recognize as poetry) with lines of varying length and considerable white space on every page will appeal to reluctant readers. Read aloud pages 1–3, where the scene is set and the murder is described. Glenn's *The Taking of Room 114: A Hostage Drama in Poems* (Lodestar Books, 1997) and *Jump Ball: A Basketball Season in Poems* (Lodestar Books, 1997) are excellent companion books.

Booktalks

On the Spot

He's a teacher . . . he's a runner . . . and he's dead. *Who Killed Mr. Chippendale?* A student? Another teacher? Who?

With the Author's Words

> In the early morning light,
> Robert Chippendale, English teacher
> For more than twenty years at Tower High,
> Punches in at 7:04.
> He will never touch the card again.

> *He is unaware that before this day, February 27, is over,*
> *Tower will be rocked by murder. (p. 1)*

Mr. Chippendale's murder. *Who Killed Mr. Chippendale?*

Literature Extensions/Alternative Book Report Activities

Sociology/Teen Issues—*Who Killed Mr. Chippendale?* touches on many controversial issues in the lives of contemporary teenagers—sex, drugs, violence, relationships, and so on. Prompt an examination of these issues with respect to your school. What is the current situation, and what steps are being taken to help students in need? Talk about community resources that are available to help teens with problems. Encourage student discussion and writing using the following books as examples: *Speaking Out: Teenagers Take on Race, Sex, and Identity* by Susan Kuklin (G. P. Putnam's Sons, 1993); *Ask Me if I Care: Voices from an American High School* by Nancy J. Rubin (Ten Speed Press, 1994); *Voices from the Street* by S. Beth Atkin (Little, Brown and Company, 1996); and *Coming of Age: The True Adventures of Two American Teens* by G. Wayne Miller (Random House, 1995).

Current Events/Sociology/Murder in Schools/Internet—The death of Mr. Chippendale is closely related to the New York City death of teacher Jonathan Levin, who was killed in 1997 by a former student. This does not seem to be an isolated incident. By searching such Internet news sites as *Time* at http://pathfinder.com/, *The New York Times* at http://www.nytimes.com/, and *USA Today* at http://www.usatoday.com/, students can research the circumstances and the frequency concerning these types of crimes. Expand the topic to other violent crimes that occur in schools. What conclusions can students draw by analyzing different cases?

Drama/Readers' Theater/Internet—The simple format of readers' theater matches the style of this spare novel. Students can adapt *Who Killed Mr. Chippendale?* to a readers' theater script featuring the seven main characters and consolidating the voices of the forty-five other characters who are briefly featured. Glenn's work was inspired by *Spoon River Anthology*, the classic 1915 collection of dramatic monologues by Edgar Lee Masters. (Annotated edition, University of Illinois Press, 1992.) Provide that work and also consult Aaron Shepard's "Readers on Stage: Tips for Reader's Theater" at http://www.aaronshep.com/rt/ROS.html for "an online guide to scripting, staging, and performing."

Sociology/Teen Issues/Violence—Violence is a growing problem facing many communities and high schools. Focus on this issue by researching specific incidents or by directing student inquiry toward a more global perspective. Reading aloud the picture book *Just One Flick of a Finger,* written by Marybeth Lorbiecki and illustrated by David Diaz (Dial Books for Young Readers, 1996), will quickly introduce this topic and help launch a discussion.

Student/Teacher Books

Been Clever Forever by Bruce Stone

A Begonia for Miss Applebaum by Paul Zindel

Here at the Scenic-Vu Motel by Thelma Hatch Wyss

Is That You, Miss Blue? by M. E. Kerr

Killing Mr. Griffin by Lois Duncan

Nothing but the Truth: A Documentary Novel by Avi

Owl in Love by Patrice Kindl

Probably Still Nick Swansen by Virginia Wolff

Sydney, Herself by Colby Rodowsky

The Taking of Room 114: A Hostage Drama in Poems by Mel Glenn

Up the Down Staircase by Bel Kaufman

Wart, Son of Toad by Alden R. Carter

Who Killed Mr. Chippendale? by Mel Glenn

Is This Your High School?

Beyond the Chocolate War by Robert Cormier

The Boy Who Owned the School by Gary Paulsen

Chocolate War by Robert Cormier

Game Plan by Thomas J. Dygard

Locked Out by Margaret Yang

Nothing but the Truth: A Documentary Novel by Avi

A Semester in the Life of a Garbage Bag by Gordon Korman

Slave Day by Rob Thomas

The Taking of Room 114: A Hostage Drama in Poems by Mel Glenn

Who Killed Mr. Chippendale? by Mel Glenn

Poetry

Angelou, Maya. *Life Doesn't Frighten Me.* Paintings by Jean-Michel Basquiat

Beatty, Paul. *Joker, Joker, Deuce*

Cool Salsa: Bilingual Poems on Growing Up Latino in the United States. Ed. by Lori M. Carlson

Medearis, Angela Shelf. *Skin Deep and Other Teenage Reflections*

Merriam, Eve. *The Inner City Mother Goose.* Illus. by David Diaz

Moser, Barry. *Polly Vaughn*

Noyes, Alfred. *The Highwayman.* Illus. by Neil Waldman

Poetry in Motion: One Hundred Poems from the Subways & Buses. Ed. by Elise Paschen et al.

Rylant, Cynthia. *Something Permanent*

Service, Robert. *The Shooting of Dan McGrew.* Illus. by Ted Harrison

Strauss, Gwen. *Trail of Stones*

Tennyson, Alfred. *The Lady of Shalott.* Illus. by Charles Keeping

Koertge, Ron
Confess-O-Rama

LC 96-5748. 1996. 165p. $16.95 (ISBN 0-531-08865-0). Orchard Books. 1998. $4.50pa. (ISBN 0-440-22713-5.). Laurel Leaf.

Genres: Contemporary realistic fiction, humor

Themes: Mothers and sons, interpersonal relations, death, moving, grief, high school life, artists, art, confession, peer pressure, health foods, step parents, therapy, sexual harassment, censorship, cooking, funerals, handicaps

Reading level: Fifth grade

Interest level: Seventh through twelfth grade

Reviews:
The Book Report. 15(5):37 March/April 1997.
Booklist. 93(3):342 October 1, 1996.
Bulletin of the Center for Children's Books. 50(3):103 November 1996. (Recommended and starred)
School Library Journal. 42(9):227 September 1996. (Starred review)

Author Information

Ron Koertge (pronounced Kur-chee) was born in Illinois and graduated from the University of Illinois and the University of Arizona. When he was a teenager, Koertge discovered he had a "way with words" and went on to write poetry in graduate school. At first Koertge tried writing adult novels, but a friend recommended the young adult market, which, he thought, matched Koertge's frank and irreverent style. Koertge currently is a professor of English at Pasadena City College in California.

Plot Summary

It's another new school for fifteen-year-old Tony, who has his hands full caring for his grieving mother whose fourth husband has just died. Passionate about cooking and worried about his mom, Tony thinks he is indifferent to peer pressure and finding new friends. But he can't resist dialing Confess-O-Rama, a strange hotline that invites callers to state their troubles and hang up. Tony thought his irreverent and sometimes humorous confessions were private and anonymous—that was, until his new quirky, artistic girlfriend Jordan reveals that Confess-O-Rama is her latest project.

Introducing the Book

Many students can identify with the "new kid in school" scenario. Capture ready-made interest by booktalking or reading aloud the section beginning with "Hey! Hey, new boy! Check this out" down to "*Oh, man.*" (pp. 16–17, hardback edition)

Booktalks

On the Spot

Who could resist an opportunity to tell all your troubles to an anonymous recording? How could it backfire? It's unusual and free and easy and safe. It's Confess-O-Rama, and it's definitely *not* a secret!

With the Author's Words

(Prop: Create the flier described on page 14 hardback edition.)
Tony sees this Confess-O-Rama flier:

> *Why hold it all in?*
> *Confession's good for the soul. Call and spill your guts*
> *to a sympathetic machine. No names, no taboos.*
> *Anonymity guaranteed. So tell me everything!*

Later he discovers the phone number tucked away in his pocket, and he calls. This funny book will tell you all about the guts Tony spills and the weird friends he makes. It's all in *Confess-O-Rama.*

Literature Extensions/Alternative Book Report Activities

Art History/Dadaism—Jordan takes Tony to an art show featuring Dada art. The name Dada is intentionally meaningless and refers to an anti-art movement that took place from 1915 to 1922 and led to the advent of surrealism in the 1920s. The focus was on experimental and irrational activities, such as automatic drawing, nonsense poetry, and "noise music." Students can find out more about this outrageous and interesting time in art history and perhaps create something in that style.

Rob Thomas's recent young adult novel *Rats Saw God* (Simon & Schuster Books for Young People, 1996) also features young people involved in Dadaism. Perhaps a revival is in the offing?

Current Events/Sexual Harassment/First Amendment—The focus is on two major issues—sexual harassment and First Amendment rights—when Jordan's dart board bra is created and worn to express her outrage at being sexually harassed by boys at her school. " 'Take a good look,' she said. 'These darts are what it feels like to have someone like you ogle my boobs five days of the week.' " (p. 135, hardback edition) When Jordan is ordered to leave the school, she insists her rights to free speech are being violated.

What do students think? Students can find information on both issues by researching newspapers, periodicals, and the Internet. Assign an essay, stage a debate, or have a lively classroom discussion!

Communication/Media/Radio & Television—Larry, the radio talk show host, is interested in starting a high school talk radio show featuring students and student issues. A forum like this could be started or may already be available in your community. Encourage students to be involved in broadcasting their own talk shows. In addition to radio, check out local community access television stations that are eager to train students and provide equipment, studio, and airtime for teen use.

Sociology/Customs/Funerals/Internet—Tony's mother is hired by a mortuary; after all, she feels she is an expert after burying four husbands. Students can learn more about the often-neglected topics of death and funerals. Guide students to the consumer resources and brochures of the "National Funeral Directors Association" at http://www.nfda.org/resources/index.html; *Corpses, Coffins, and Crypts* by Penny Colman (Henry Holt and Company, 1997); and the classic *The American Way of Death* by Jessica Mitford (Simon & Schuster, 1963).

For Laughing Out Loud!

Bauer, Joan. *Squashed*

Gilmore, Kate. *Enter Three Witches*

Koertge, Ron. *Confess-O-Rama*

Koertge, Ron. *Harmony Arms*

Korman, Gordon. *Don't Care High*

Korman, Gordon. *Losing Joe's Place*

Powell, Randy. *Is Kissing a Girl Who Smokes Like Licking an Ashtray?*

Rodowsky, Colby. *Sydney, Herself*

Sleator, William. *Oddballs*

Dealing with Death . . . in YA Fiction

Allen. R. E. *Ozzy on the Outside*

Brooks, Martha. *Two Moons in August*

Carter, Alden R. *Wart, Son of Toad*

Deaver, Julie Reece. *You Bet Your Life*

Donovan, Stacey. *Dive*

Grant, Cynthia D. *Shadow Man*

Johnson, Angela. *Toning the Sweep*

Johnston, Julie. *Adam and Eve and Pinch Me*

Klause, Annette Curtis. *The Silver Kiss*

Koertge, Ron. *Confess-O-Rama*

Lynch, Chris. *Shadow Boxer*

McDaniel Lurlene. *Don't Die, My Love*

Sauer, Jim. *Hank*

Guys 'n Love

Clements, Bruce. *Tom Loves Anna Loves Tom*

Gilmore, Kate. *Enter Three Witches*

Greene, Constance. *The Love Letters of J. Thomas Owen*

Koertge, Ron. *Boy in the Moon*

Koertge, Ron. *Confess-O-Rama*

Mazer, Harry. *The Girl of His Dreams*

Mazer, Harry. *I Love You, Stupid!*

Peck, Richard. *Those Summer Girls I Never Met*

Thomas, Rob. *Rats Saw God*

Wersba, Barbara. *The Farewell Kid*

Lester, Julius

Othello: A Novel

LC 94-12833. 1995. 151p. $12.95 (ISBN 0-590-41967-6). Scholastic.
1998. 160p. $3.99pa. (ISBN 0-590-41966-8). Scholastic Point.

Genres: Historical fiction, multicultural

Themes: Love; Shakespeare, William (1564–1616); passion; prejudice; racism; deception; jealousy; tragedy; betrayal; soldiers; interracial marriage; dramas; plays

Reading level: Upper sixth grade

Interest level: Eighth through twelfth grade

Reviews:
The Book Report. 13(5):38 March/April 1995.

Booklist. 91(12):1074 February 15, 1995. (Boxed review)
Bulletin of the Center for Children's Books. 48(7):241–42 March 1995. (Recommended)
Publishers Weekly. 242(12):62 March 20, 1995.
School Library Journal. 41(4):154 April 1995. (Starred review)
Voice of Youth Advocates. 18(4):96 June 1995. (#3 quality, #2 popularity)

Author Information

Julius Lester's love of storytelling began with his Methodist minister father, who was noted for his stories. At various times in his life, Lester has been a singer, a professional musician, a Civil Rights activist, a radio announcer, and a professor. Well known for his collections of African American folktales, Lester finds it rewarding to write about his African American heritage. According to Lester's online interview for "Amazon.com," he has been using the Internet for four or five years to participate in discussions about children's literature, communicate with editors, and do research. He's a stamp collector, a mystery reader, and he likes to cook.

The idea for reworking *Othello* occurred when he was contemplating putting together a collection of love stories from a variety of cultures. Abandoning that project, Lester decided instead to retell as much of Shakespeare as he could. He plans to work next on *The Merchant of Venice* and then on *Romeo and Juliet*.

Plot Summary

The setting is sixteenth-century England instead of Venice; the genre is a novel rather than a play; but the story of *Othello* is the familiar tragedy of passionate love, jealousy, and evil. Lester has reimagined the play, still looking at race as a critical theme. Othello, Iago, and Emilia (Emily) are all Africans, and Desdemona's father is an English king. Duped by Iago into believing that Desdemona is unfaithful, Othello kills her and then slays himself after learning of Iago's treachery.

Introducing the Book

The great cover art, tragic love-story theme, larger-than-usual typeset, and wide margins combine to make this twenty-three-chapter book appealing to reluctant teen Shakespeare readers. Skip the introduction until after the story is read. (Lester's explanation of why and how he created the book is useful and interesting for the teacher beforehand; students will appreciate it after reading the book.) Read aloud to "What do you want her to know?" (p. 31, hardback edition) to get readers started.

This book can serve as a bridge to the play, not as a replacement. Lester emphasized different aspects of the story—especially the issue of racism. *Othello,* edited by Roma Gill (Oxford University Press, 1994), and *Shakespeare: To Teach or Not to Teach* by Cass Foster and Lynn Johnson (Five Star Publishers, 1992) can be of assistance to those who have to teach Shakespeare but are not totally comfortable with the works.

Booktalks

On the Spot

This *Othello* may not exactly match Shakespeare's original tragedy, but Shakespeare would definitely approve of the romance, passion, and jealousy surrounding a brave warrior and his beautiful wife.

With the Author's Words

Othello and Desdemona are deeply in love, but enemies plot against them and would like to see their passion undone. The seed of jealousy has been planted.

"My lord?" she whispered, her voice scarcely audible. Perhaps it was the softness in her voice, but, as awakening from a dream, he saw the fear in her face. What was he doing that the one he loved more than life should now be afraid of him? (pp. 116–17, hardback edition)

Literature Extensions/Alternative Book Report Activities

Creative Writing/Adaptations—Shakespeare's original *Othello* was probably an adaptation of an Italian novel. Lester's *Othello* is an adaptation of Shakespeare's play. When Shakespeare and Lester wrote their adaptations, they did so using their own styles, emphasizing characteristics important to their time and culture.

Keeping this information in mind, invite students to write their own adaptations of traditional tales, such as "The Three Little Pigs," "The Frog Prince," "Little Red Riding Hood," or wordless picture books, such as *Across Town* by Sara (Orchard Books, 1991) and *The Grey Lady and the Strawberry Snatcher* by Molly Bang (Four Winds Press, 1980).

Drama/Film Festivals/Internet—Put together a Shakespeare film festival, beginning with *The Tragedy of Othello: The Moor of Venice,* directed by Orson Welles (Mercury Productions, 1952). (This classic was re-released in video format in the 1990s.) Include such current films as Kenneth Branagh's four-hour production of *Hamlet* (Castle Rock Entertainment/Columbia Pictures, 1996), which features an eclectic cast of well-known contemporary actors; *Rosencrantz and Guildenstern Are Dead* (1990), a modern comedy featuring two minor characters from *Hamlet*; *Romeo & Juliet* (Twentieth Century Fox, 1996), a surreal retelling set in a modern suburb of Verona; and *Looking for Richard* (20th Century Fox, 1996), Al Pacino's film with scenes from the play juxtaposed against rehearsals, discussions, and actor interviews.

For a complete and up-to-date list of Shakespeare movies for a film festival, conduct a "writer" search at "The Internet Movie Database" at http://us.imdb.com/search.

Drama/Acting/Internet—Several Internet sites provide assistance in acting and producing Shakespearean dramas. Access lessons about various areas of acting (characterization, fundamentals, improvisation, movement and mannerisms, directing, costumes, scene development, and so forth) at http://www.byu.edu/tmcbucs/arts-ed/units/unithome.html and "Ideas for Teaching Shakespeare Through Performance" at http://www.ivgh.com/amy/teach.html.

Helpful books include *Shakespeare Set Free: Teaching Twelfth Night and Othello,* edited by Peggy O'Brien (Washington Square Press, 1995) and *The Sixty Minute Shakespeare* acting editions by Cass Foster (Five Star Publishers, 1997).

History/Slave Trade/Internet—A combination of books and Internet sites can make a study of the African slave trade come alive. Introduce students to *The Middle Passage: White Ship/Black Cargo* by Tom Feeling (Dial, 1995) and *Spirits of the Passage: The Transatlantic Slave Trade in the Seventeenth Century* by Madeleine Burnside (Simon & Schuster, 1997). Then explore the links at "William Bosman's Description of the African Slave Trade, 1701" from the University of Wisconsin History Network at http://vi.uh.edu/pages/mintz/primary.htm.

Love Stories with a Twist

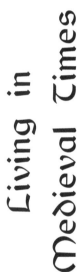

Cooney, Caroline B. *Both Sides of Time*

Cooney, Caroline B. *Out of Time*

Cooney, Caroline B. *The Stranger*

Cormier, Robert. *We All Fall Down*

Davis, Jenny. *Sex Education*

Kindl, Patrice. *Owl in Love*

Klause, Annette Curtis. *Blood and Chocolate*

Klause, Annette Curtis. *The Silver Kiss*

Lester, Julius. *Othello*

Mahy, Margaret. *The Changeover: A Supernatural Romance*

Rylant, Cynthia. *A Couple of Kooks and Other Stories About Love*

Living in Medieval Times

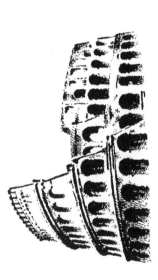

Cushman, Karen. *Catherine, Called Birdy*

Cushman, Karen. *The Midwife's Apprentice*

Garden, Nancy. *Dove and Sword*

Konigsburg, E. L. *A Proud Taste of Scarlet Miniver*

Lester, Julius. *Othello*

McKinley, Robin. *The Outlaws of Sherwood*

Pope, Elizabeth. *The Perilous Guard*

Skurzynski, Gloria. *Manwolf*

Stanley, Diane. *Bard of Avon: The Story of William Shakespeare*

Temple, Frances. *The Ramsay Scallop*

Tomlinson, Theresa. *The Forestwife*

Alternative Shakespeare

Avi. *Romeo and Juliet Together (And Alive!) at Last*

Beneduce, Ann Keay. *The Tempest*

Coville, Bruce. *Macbeth*

Coville, Bruce. *A Midsummer Night's Dream*

Coville, Bruce. *The Tempest*

Foster, Cass. *The Sixty-Minute Shakespeare: Romeo and Juliet*

Garfield, Leon. *Shakespeare Stories*

Garfield, Leon. *Shakespeare Stories II*

Lamb, Charles, and Mary Lamb. *Tales from Shakespeare*

McCaughrean, Geraldine. *Stories from Shakespeare*

Nesbit, E. *The Best of Shakespeare*

Ross, Stewart. *Shakespeare and Macbeth: The Story Behind the Play*

Macaulay, David

Rome Antics

LC 97-20941. 1997. 79p. $18.00 (ISBN 0-395-82289-3). Houghton Mifflin.

Genres: Picture books, nonfiction, humor, romance

Themes: Rome, homing pigeons, buildings—historic, perspective, point of view, flying, flight, line, color, messages, tour, travelogue, architecture, ruins, modern cities, maps, love, romance, puns

Reading level: Eighth grade

Interest level: All ages

Reviews:
Bulletin of the Center for Children's Books. 51(4):133 December 1997. (Recommended)
Horn Book. 74(1):66 January/February 1998.
Publishers Weekly. 244(37):76 October 8, 1997. (Starred review)
School Library Journal. 43(11):121 November 1997. (Starred review)

Author Information

David Macaulay encourages students to "ask themselves why things look the way they do." He uses words and illustration to "demystify an increasingly complex and detached world." Raised in Lancashire, England, Macaulay was encouraged to create and develop projects constantly. His parents made everything from sweaters to easels, and Macaulay says he and his siblings were brought up to believe "that creativity and craftsmanship were desirable—even normal." Moving from England to New Jersey when he was eleven was a shock for Macaulay, but his imagination never faltered. He attended the Rhode Island School of Design to study architecture but later moved into painting and illustration.

Plot Summary

While a homing pigeon carries a message to a person in Rome, the reader gets an adventurous bird's eye tour of the ancient ruins, cultural landmarks, and modern life in the city. The afterword, "Rome: As the Pigeon Flies," includes in-depth notes on each of the twenty-two buildings featured in the story.

Introducing the Book

Although this large book could be initially shared aloud, the intricate architectural drawings require up-close exploration. This book is filled with visual humor and playful language. The numerous visual clues offset the high reading level that is heavily influenced by the afterword.

Booktalks

On the Spot

All roads may lead to Rome, but the pigeon in this book definitely does *not* stay on the road *or* take the shortest route. Her erratic flight path leads to danger, adventure, and, just maybe, the delivery of an important message.

With the Author's Words

> *As she approaches an abandoned gatehouse, a most unprofessional thought enters her head. Instead of traveling directly to her destination, which is standard pigeon procedure, she decides to take the scenic route. In no time she is circling the most famous amphitheater in the world . . . .*
> *(pp. 9–13, hardback edition)*

It's the Coliseum! And now, in no time she'll be spiraling through the ruins and falling catty-wampus toward some other architectural wonder. Will her important message ever be delivered? And, just what is this message, anyway? The answer is the title—*Rome Antics*.

Literature Extensions/Alternative Book Report Activities

Architecture/Community Project—David Macaulay is well known for his books featuring architecture, including *Castle* (Houghton Mifflin, 1977); *Cathedral: The Story of Its Construction* (Houghton Mifflin, 1973); and *Pyramid: The Story of Its Construction* (Houghton Mifflin, 1975). To introduce architecture to your students, provide these books along with *Architecture* by Neil Stevenson (DK Publishing, 1997); *Architects Make Zigzags: Looking at Architecture from A to Z* by Roxie Munro (Preservation Press, 1986); *Stephen Biesty's Incredible Cross-Sections* by Richard Platt (Alfred A. Knopf, 1992); and *Round Buildings, Square Buildings, & Buildings That Wiggle Like a Fish* by Philip M. Isaacson (Alfred A. Knopf, 1988), a picture book glossary of architectural terms.

Using *Rome Antics* as a model, students can explore the architecture in their area. They can photograph or illustrate different buildings from unique perspectives (think of the pigeon!) and focus on interesting architectural details. The final project could be displayed at the local chamber of commerce or public library.

Art/Line and Color—The basic elements of art include line, color, value (also called light and dark), shape, texture, and space. In her article "Illustration as Art: Line" (*Book Links* 4[3]:54–57 January 1995), Barbara Elleman explains, "the angle, the width, the length, and the motion of a line are what an artist uses to express what he or she wants to say, much like a writer makes use of verbs, adjectives, and adverbs." (p. 54) Use this article, as well as another Elleman article, "Illustration as Art: Color" (*Book Links* 4[5]:58–61 May 1995); the references she cites; and *Art and Design in Children's Picture Books: An Analysis of Caldecott Award-Winning Illustrations* by Lyn Ellen Lacy (American Library Association, 1986) for more information about the uses of line and color by artists.

Macaulay's use of line in *Rome Antics* is both subtle and dramatic. His architectural renderings are created with his signature pen-and-ink drawings, and the dramatic red line leads the reader's eye around the pages and through the story. Use *Rome Antics* along with *Bad Day at Riverbend* by Chris Van Allsburg (Houghton Mifflin, 1995); *Hush! A Thai Lullaby* by Minfong Ho and illustrated by Holly Meade (Orchard Books, 1996); and *The Squiggle* by Carole Lexa Schaefer and illustrated by Pierr Morgan (Crown, 1996), for contrasting and comparing the similarities and differences in the illustrators' use of red line. Using the artwork of these four artists as an example, students can experiment with line and color themselves.

Hobbies/Pigeons—Raising homing pigeons has been a popular hobby for decades. Invite an expert to speak to students about this hobby, or provide some of the following books for further research: *Aloft: A Meditation on Pigeons and Pigeon-Flying* by Stephen Bodio (Lyons & Burford Publishers, 1990); *Pigeons and Doves* by Ray Nofsinger and Jim Hargrove (Childrens Press, 1992); and Jane Kurtz's Ethiopian tale about homing pigeons entitled *Only a Pigeon* (Simon & Schuster, 1997).

Travel/Geography/Economics—For people, traveling to Rome certainly involves more than a red line. Students can plan a trip abroad to Rome or another destination. Their assignment can include obtaining a passport, establishing a travel budget, making flight reservation, developing a tour plan, and the like. Local travel agents, the public library, and the Internet are all valuable resources.

Great Picture Books for Older Readers! A Picture Is Worth a Thousand Words

Baille, Allan. *Rebel*

Burleigh, Robert. *Hoops*

Cooper, Roscoe. *The Diary of Victor Frankenstein*

Fox, Mem. *Feathers and Fools*

Garland, Sherry. *I Never Knew Your Name*

Myers, Walter Dean. *Harlem*

Robinson, Aminah Brenda Lynn. *A Street Called Home*

Sis, Peter. *Starry Messenger: Galileo Galilei*

Spohn, Kate. *Broken Umbrellas*

Taylor, Clark. *The House That Crack Built*

Thompson, Colin. *How to Live Forever*

Wood, Audrey. *Bright and Early Thursday Evening: A Tangled Tale*

Wood, Michele. *Going Back Home: An Artist Returns to the South*

Young, Ed. *Voices of the Heart*

Presenting David Macaulay!

Baaa (c1985)

Black and White (c1990)

Castle (c1983)

Cathedral (c1985)

City (c1974)

Mill (c1983)

Motel of the Mysteries (c1979)

Pyramid (c1975)

Roman City (c1994)

Rome Antics (c1997)

Ship (c1993)

Unbuilding (c1980)

Underground (c1976)

The Way Things Work (c1988)

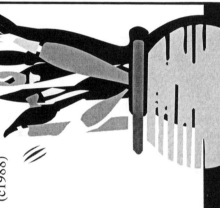

"City Tours" by Picture Books & Company

Brown, Tricia. *The City by the Bay: A Magical Journey Around San Francisco*

French, Fiona. *Snow White in New York*

Hernandez, Xavier, and Jordi Ballonga. *Lebek: A City of Northern Europe Through the Ages*

Hernandez, Xavier, and Pilar Comes. *Barmi: A Mediterranean City Through the Ages*

Jakobsen, Kathy. *My New York*

Munro, Roxie. *The Inside-Outside Book of London*

Munro, Roxie. *The Inside-Outside Book of New York*

Munro, Roxie. *The Inside-Outside Book of Paris*

Munro, Roxie. *The Inside-Outside Book of Washington, D.C.*

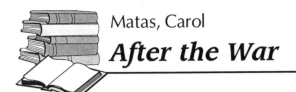

Matas, Carol
After the War

LC 95-43613. 1996. 115p. $16.00 (ISBN 0-689-80350-8). Simon & Schuster Books for Young Readers. 1997. 133p. $4.50pa. (ISBN 0-689-80722-8). Aladdin Paperbacks.

Genres: Historical fiction, adventure, multicultural

Themes: Holocaust, Jews, Zionism, children, escape, survival, hope, courage, mobs, pogroms, love, smuggling, violence, orphans, immigrants, fears, stories, Palestine, World War II

Reading level: Sixth grade

Interest level: Sixth through twelfth grade

Reviews:
The Book Report. 15(4):35 January/February 1997.
Booklist. 92(15):1361 April 1, 1996. (Starred review)
Bulletin of the Center for Children's Books. 49(8):271 April 1996.
Publishers Weekly. 239(23):72 May 18, 1996.
School Library Journal. 42(5):135 May 1996.

Author Information

Carol Matas lives with her husband and two children in Winnipeg, Canada. Although she intended to become an actor, Matas began writing children's books while raising her family and found herself well-suited to this profession because it gave her an opportunity to make a difference. Well known for her historical fiction featuring young adult protagonists facing complex and dangerous situations, Matas likes to focus on heroism and give readers something about which to think. Many of her novels are set during World War II, a time period that, for Matas, offers dramatic adventure stories featuring characters faced with moral dilemmas.

Plot Summary

Returning to her Polish village after the liberation of Buchenwald at the end of World War II, fifteen-year-old Ruth is unable to find any surviving family members. Wandering aimlessly, Ruth is taken in by members of a underground organization who request her help to smuggle illegal immigrant children into Palestine. Ruth's personal struggle to find hope parallels her risky trip across Europe taking orphans to Palestine. Ruth's story continues in *The Garden* (Simon & Schuster, 1997).

Introducing the Book

Reading aloud the first chapter of *After the War* will hook many potential readers because heart-wrenching, vivid Holocaust survival stories are favorites of many teens.

Booktalks

On the Spot

It seems unlikely that a fifteen-year-old could smuggle orphans across Europe, but it's true. This story is based on real events *After the War*—World War II.

With the Author's Words

When we lived in the ghetto Hannah often begged me to tell them stories at night. But I couldn't think of anything scarier than real life anymore. Especially after the day most of the Jews were herded into the town square and shot. Father hid us under the floorboards of the house we were staying in. Others had escaped somehow, too. Those of us who lived were put to work in factories. Until we too were taken away. (p. 3, hardback edition)

And now the war is over. After losing her entire family in the concentration camps, Ruth can see little reason to go on. Why not smuggle orphans and risk her own life? What will happen to Ruth . . . *After the War*?

Literature Extensions/Alternative Book Report Activities

Current Events/Middle East/Palestinians and Jews/Debate—The conclusion of *After the War* is based on the history of Zionists and their immigration to Israel. Provide Otto Preminger's 1960 movie *Exodus* (United Artists, 1960) and the novel it was based on, *Exodus* by Leon Uris (reissue edition, Bantam Books, 1983) for further information. These presentations will help orient students to the current conflict in the Middle East between the Palestinians and the Jews.

Using the Internet and traditional research resources, students can identify the history of the conflict, the peace negotiations, and hope for a settlement in the future. This is an ideal topic for classic debate where students must be able to defend both sides of an issue.

For a fictional presentation of the Palestinian perspective, provide students with *Habibi* by Naomi Shihab Nye (Simon & Schuster Books for Young Readers, 1997).

History/Holocaust/Internet—In addition to the traditional print resources, the Internet can provide students with informative visual and written information about the Holocaust. Encourage further research at both the "Remember" organization at http://remember.org/cylinks.html, which provides numerous links to museums and memorials around the world, a virtual tour of Auschwitz, survivors online, a teachers' guide, lesson plans, and bibliographies, and the "United States Holocaust Memorial Museum" in Washington, D.C., at http://www.ushmm.org. Also provide *The World Must Know: The History of the Holocaust as Told in the United States Holocaust Memorial Museum* by Michael Berenbaum (Little, Brown and Company, 1993).

History/Horror of War/Children/Biographies/Internet—A plethora of material is available for continued student research and reading about the Holocaust as well as information about the effect of war upon children. A million and a half children and teenagers were among the victims of the Holocaust. The powerful "Children of the Holocaust" site at http://www.wiesenthal.com/children/prvchild.htm, sponsored by the Museum of Tolerance in Los Angeles, provides access to more than 120 biographies (including photographs) and facts about these children. Likewise, *Tell Them We Remember: The Story of the Holocaust* by Susan D. Bachrach (Little, Brown and Company, 1994), is based on the information and artifacts at the United States Holocaust Memorial Museum. Photographs of young adults and written excerpts from museum "identification cards" put a human face on the Holocaust for many students today.

Other books about children and war include: *Bosnia: Civil War in Europe* (from the Children in Crisis series) by John Isaac and Keith Elliot Greenberg (Blackbirch Marketing, 1996); *Children in the Holocaust and World War II: Their Secret Diaries* by Laurel Holliday (Pocket Books, 1995); *We Are Witnesses* by Jacob Boas (Henry Holt and Company, 1995); *The Boys' War: Confederate and Union Soldiers Talk About the Civil War* by Jim Murphy (Clarion Books, 1993); *The Hidden Children* by Howard Greenfeld (Ticknor & Fields, 1993); *Hiding to Survive: Stories of Jewish Children Rescued from the Holocaust* by Maxine B. Rosenberg (Clarion Books, 1994); *Shin's Tricycle* by Tatsuharu Kodama (Walker & Company, 1995); *Zalata's Diary: A Child's Life in Sarajevo* by Zalata Filipovic (Viking, 1994); *I Never Saw Another Butterfly: Children's Drawings and Poems from Terezin Concentration Camp, 1942–1944,* edited by Hana Volavkova (Schocken Books, 1993); *The Diary of a Young Girl: The Definitive Edition* by Anne Frank (Doubleday, 1995); and *Anne Frank: Beyond the Diary: A Photographic Remembrance* by Ruud Van Der Rol (Viking, 1993).

Classroom Collection/Picture Books/Holocaust—The Holocaust has been vividly portrayed in numerous picture books suitable for older readers. These short, evocative books can provide an introduction to a study of this subject. They include: *The Children We Remember* by Chana Byers Abells (Greenwillow Books, 1983, 1986); *Hilde and Eli: Children of the Holocaust* by David Adler (Holiday House, 1994); *Star of Fear, Star of Hope* by Jo Hoestlandt (Walker & Company, 1995); *My Brother's Keeper: The Holocaust Through the Eyes of an Artist* by Israel Bernbaum (G. P. Putnam's Sons, 1985); *Terrible Things: An Allegory of the Holocaust* by Eve Bunting (Jewish Publication Society, 1989); *Let the Celebrations Begin!* by Margaret Wild (Orchard Books, 1991); *Rose Blanche* by Roberto Innocenti (Creative Education, 1985); and *The Number on My Grandfather's Arm* by David A. Adler (UAHC Press, 1987).

Escape Stories

Bunting, Eve. *How Many Days to America? A Thanksgiving Story*

Choi, Sook Nyul. *The Year of Impossible Goodbyes*

Friedman, Carl. *Nightfather*

Friedman, Ina R. *Escape or Die: True Stories of Young People Who Survived the Holocaust*

Garland, Sherry. *The Lotus Seed*

Kherdian, David. *The Road from Home: The Story of an Armenian Girl*

Lasky, Kathryn. *The Night Journey*

Lowry, Lois. *Number the Stars*

Matas, Carol. *After the War*

Paulsen, Gary. *Nightjohn*

Perl, Lila, and Marion Blumenthal. *Four Perfect Pebbles: A Holocaust Story*

Watkins, Yoko Kawashima. *So Far from the Bamboo Grove*

The Holocaust— The Truth

Frank, Anne. *Anne Frank: The Diary of a Young Girl*

Gilbert, Martin. *The Holocaust: A History of the Jews of Europe During the Second World War*

Ippisch, Hanneke. *Sky: A True Story of Resistance During World War II*

Meltzer, Milton. *Never to Forget: The Jews of the Holocaust*

Novac, Ana. *The Beautiful Days of My Youth: My Six Months in Auschwitz and Plaszow*

Rogasky, Barbara. *Smoke and Ashes: The Story of the Holocaust*

Holocaust Fiction

Ackerman, Karen. *The Night Crossing*

Gehrts, Barbara. *Don't Say a Word*

Laird, Christa. *Shadow of the Wall*

Lingard, Joan. *Tug of War*

Matas, Carol. *After the War*

Nolan, Hal. *If I Should Die Before I Wake*

O'Neil, Denny, and Michael Kaluta. *The Shadow*

Ramati, Alexander. *And the Violins Stopped Playing: A Story of the Gypsy Holocaust*

Temperley, Alan. *Murdo's War*

Westall, Robert. *Blitzcat*

Yolen, Jane. *Devil's Arithmetic*

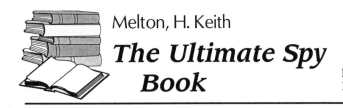

Melton, H. Keith

The Ultimate Spy Book

LC 95-44054. 1996. 176p. $29.95 (ISBN 0-7894-0443-5). Dorling Kindersley.

Genre: Nonfiction

Themes: Espionage, spies, spying, defense, collections, weapons, defectors, sabotage, assassins, surveillance, drugs, codes, eavesdropping, escape, intelligence agencies, cameras, satellite surveillance, recruitment

Reading level: Ninth grade

Interest level: Fifth grade and up

Reviews:
School Library Journal. 42(7):109 July 1996.
Voice of Youth Advocates. 19(4):234–35 October 1996. (#4 quality, #4 popularity)

Author Information

A well-known military historian and an expert on spies and spying, H. Keith Melton is a recognized authority on espionage devices. A noted collector, Melton has put together an assortment of papers, spying equipment, and books. Melton is also an expert on historical espionage equipment and serves as an adviser to U.S. intelligence agencies. He also serves on the board of advisers of the National Historical Intelligence Museum in Washington, D.C.

Plot Summary

Using Dorling Kindersley's signature double-page spreads, Melton provides an account of the profession of international espionage along with a multitude of details about spy techniques and technology. He offers a historical perspective as well in sidebars detailing individual spies and their escapades, information about particular devices and their uses, codes and code-breaking, secret reports, counterintelligence, assassinations, and more.

Introducing the Book

One reviewer notes, "I had students begging for the book before I finished reading it" (*Voice of Youth Advocates*). This interesting book will not need selling even though the reading level is high due to the technical terminology. The multitude of picture information and clues make up for the high reading level.

Booktalks

On the Spot

Enter the clandestine world of spying and learn some of the best-kept secrets of espionage. The truth, stranger than fiction, is in *The Ultimate Spy Book*!

With the Author's Words

Listen to this! A British agent in World War II . . .

> *codenamed Garbo . . . was so successful in deceiving the Germans on behalf of the Allies that he was decorated by both sides! (p. 11)*

Could Garbo have been *the* ultimate spy? Find out by investigating *The Ultimate Spy Book*.

Literature Extensions/Alternative Book Report Activities

Careers/Spying—Many students will be interested in the following books just because the subject of spies and espionage is fascinating to adolescents. Others may actually be interested in pursuing a career in intelligence work. Provide books such as these: *Spy Book: The Encyclopedia of Espionage* by Norman Polmar (Random House Reference, 1996); *Brassey's Book of Espionage* by John Laffin (Brassey's, Inc., 1997); *A Century of Spies: Intelligence in the Twentieth Century* by Jeffrey T. Richelson (Oxford University Press, 1995); *The Puzzle Palace: Inside the National Security Agency, America's Most Secret Intelligence Organization* by James Bamford (Penguin, 1983); *Spy* by Richard Platt (Eyewitness Books, 1996); and *Espionage: The Greatest Spy Operations of the Twentieth Century* by Ernest Volkman (John Wiley & Sons, 1995).

Communication/Codes and Ciphers—Reading or writing in secret codes is a fascination for readers of all ages. Interested students can learn more about codes and even develop one of their own. Consult such books as *Codes and Ciphers: An A to Z of Covert Communication, from the Clay Tablet to the Microdot* by Fred B. Wrixon (Macmillan, 1992); *The Cat's Elbow and Other Secret Languages* by Alvin Schwartz (Farrar, Straus & Giroux, 1988); *The Secret Code Book: With Press-Out Code-Busters* by Helen Huckle (Dial Books for Young Readers, 1995); and *Navajo Code Talkers* by Nathan Aaseng (Walker & Company, 1992).

Espionage/Internet—For current information on spying and espionage, potential modern-day sleuths can investigate the home pages of the FBI at http://www.fbi.gov/ and the CIA at http://www.odci.gov/cia/. These pages feature crime alerts, case files, speeches and testimony, information on employment, links to other sites of interest, and so on.

Vocational Education/Drafting/Inventions—Students can study "The Equipment and Techniques" section of the *Ultimate Spy Book* and view fictionalized television and movie versions of spies and spying, such as James Bond films and Max Smart (*Get Smart*) television shows. Using their imaginations, they can design, develop, and draft potential devices for future spying.

Real Spies . . .
Real Spying . . .

Axelrod, Alan. *The War Between the Spies: A History of Espionage During the American Civil War*

Clarridge, Duane R. *A Spy for All Seasons: My Life in the CIA*

Knight, Amy. *Spies Without Cloaks: The KGB's Successors*

Maas, Peter. *Killer Spy: The Inside Story of the FBI's Pursuit and Capture of Aldrich Ames, America's Deadliest Spy*

Schecter, Jerrold L. *The Spy Who Saved the World: How a Soviet Colonel Changed the Course of the Cold War*

Sullivan, George. *In the Line of Fire: Eight Women War Spies*

In This Style:

Dorling Kindersley Books

Bruce-Mitford, Miranda. *The Illustrated Book of Signs & Symbols*

Cumming, Robert. *Annotated Art*

Fogle, Bruce. *The Encyclopedia of the Cat*

Fogle, Bruce. *The Encyclopedia of the Dog*

Fry, Plantagenet Somerset. *The Dorling Kindersley History of the World*

McManners, Hugh. *The Complete Wilderness Training Book*

Melton, H. Keith. *The Ultimate Spy Book*

Pickford, Nigel. *The Atlas of Shipwrecks and Treasure*

Reid, Lori. *The Art of Hand Reading*

Willson, Quentin. *Classic American Cars*

What Are These Spies Up To?

Beatty, Patricia. *Jayhawker*

Cadnum, Michael. *Breaking the Fall*

Duncan, Lois. *Don't Look Behind You*

Lisle, Janet Taylor. *Sirens and Spies*

Matas, Carol. *Kris's War*

Myers, Walter Dean. *The Nicholas Factor*

Nixon, Joan Lowery. *A Candidate for Murder*

Rose, Malcolm. *The Highest Form of Killing*

Morris, Winifred
Liar

LC 96-2465. 1996. 161p. $15.95 (ISBN 0-8027-8461-5).
Walker & Company.

Genres: Contemporary realistic fiction, adventure

Themes: Lies, grandparents, anger, friendship, trust, choices, juvenile delinquents, juvenile justice, parenting, survival, self-discovery, bullies, truth, homesteaders, abuse, probation, fires, mothers and sons, theft, school life, farm life, homesteaders

Reading level: Fifth grade

Interest level: Sixth through eleventh grade

Reviews:
Booklist. 93(7):646 December 1, 1996.
Bulletin of the Center for Children's Books. 50(5):181 January 1997. (Recommended)
Publishers Weekly. 243(47):77 November 18, 1996.
School Library Journal. 43(1):115 January 1997.
Voice of Youth Advocates. 19(5):272 December 1996. (#3 quality, #4 popularity)

Author Information

Winifred Morris started writing when she was eight years old. She's been a high school and college teacher and, along with her husband, has "built houses, raised chickens and goats and two sons, and run a tree planting crew." *Liar* is based on a friend of Morris's who spent most of his adolescence in jail as a result of his mother's neglect. Morris writes, "much of the book also came from my younger son, who at the age of Alex had many of the same feelings as Alex—the same sense that he could do nothing right, that he was destined to fail." This son is now a self-confident musician. The setting for *Liar* is similar to Morris's own home in Oregon, an area she loves.

Plot Summary

Troubled and in trouble, fourteen-year-old city-wise Alex is given one last chance to straighten out. On probation, he's sent away from his alcoholic and neglectful mother to live with his gruff grandfather and loving grandmother on their farm. When he's falsely accused of stealing, Alex hides in an abandoned homestead where he struggles to survive during an unexpected blizzard.

Introducing the Book

Read aloud the first three chapters for a very realistic look at a troubled teen and the problems he must grapple with throughout his life. Many teens will identify with the "bad guy" image and will be hooked by the booktalks.

Booktalks

On the Spot

If your only example is a parent who rarely tells the truth, why should *you*?

With the Author's Words

Sent to live with his grandparents after years of neglect by his alcoholic mother, Alex moves into her old room.

> I was glad no one could see me like that, hugging a dumb stuffed animal. I was thinking that as if one half of my brain was seeing things from somewhere else. Somewhere rational. But with some other part of my mind, the part that is always screwing up, I pulled my knife from my pocket. I pressed the point into and through the pink fur, right into the long pink neck. "You've got to learn to manage your anger." I could almost hear Ms. Lloyd saying that to me, as I watched the white stuffing swell out behind the blade. (pp. 4–5, hardback edition)

Managing anger, telling the truth, and fitting in may all be impossible, but the alternative for Alex is juvenile detention. Will he always be a *Liar*?

Literature Extensions/Alternative Book Report Activities

Current Events/Social Issues/Juvenile Crime/Juvenile Justice/Literacy—Alex is in danger of becoming a criminal with a record if he continues to have problems. What happens to juvenile offenders in your community? What are their rights? What are typical sentences? What is the rate of juvenile crime in your community? Does your juvenile justice system incorporate the use of adolescent peer-group reviews? Working in teams or individually, have students investigate and find the answers to these questions and report back to your class.

Health/Anger Management/Conflict Resolution—Alex has trouble controlling his temper and may have benefited from anger management training, as Bo Brewster did in the novel *Ironman* by Chris Crutcher (Greenwillow Books, 1995). Mental health professionals will be delighted to visit your school to discuss helpful techniques and training centered on anger management. Provide students with pamphlets and books on this topic as well. Appropriate titles include: *Anger Management for Youth: Stemming Aggression and Violence* by Leona Eggert (National Educational Service, 1994); *Understanding and Managing Your Anger and Aggression* by Bud Nye (BCA Publications, 1993); *Straight Talk About Anger* by Christine Dentemaro and Rachel Kranz (Facts on File, 1995); and *When Anger Hurts: Quieting the Storm Within* by Matthew Mckay, et al. (New Harbinger Publications, 1989).

History/Homestead Act/Internet—Alex is intrigued when Mickey takes him to an abandoned homestead. Understanding the Homestead Act of 1862 and its impact on the development of the United States is important. Share books about homesteading, such as *Letters of a Woman Homesteader* by Elinore Pruitt Stewart (Houghton Mifflin, 1982); *My Prairie Year: Based on the Diary of Elenore Plaisted* by Brett Harvey (Holiday House, 1986); and *Settling the American West* by James Collins (Franklin Watts, 1993). On the Internet, students can read the text of the Homestead Act at http://www.pbs.org/weta/thewest/wpages/wpgs650/homestd.htm and can visit the National Park Service's "Homestead National Monument" at http://www.nps.gov/home/.

Life Skills/Survival—Alex grew up in Los Angeles and has no idea about surviving the elements in the wild. Although he plans to stay in an abandoned cabin for a while, he is ill-prepared. Every traveler needs a healthy respect for weather changes and should know basic survival skills. Have students compose a list of the items and skills Alex needed in order to survive in his situation, listing the most essential items first. Invite a speaker to present information about survival equipment and preparation for outdoor activities in the wilderness. Students can then revise their lists accordingly.

Teens & Grandparents

Grove, Vicki. *Rimwalkers*

Hamilton, Virginia. *A Little Love*

Johnson, Angela. *Toning the Sweep*

Koertge, Ron. *Tiger, Tiger Burning Bright*

Mazer, Norma Fox. *After the Rain*

Miller, Jim Wayne. *Newfound*

Morris, Winifred. *Liar*

Perkins, Mitali. *The Sunita Experiment*

Thesman, Jean. *The Rainmakers*

Voigt, Cynthia. *Dicey's Song*

Troubled Youth

Cormier, Robert. *We All Fall Down*

Crutcher, Chris. *Ironman*

Garland, Sherry. *Letters from the Mountains*

Johnston, Julie. *Adam and Eve and Pinch Me*

Lang, Susan. *Teen Violence*

Lipsyte, Robert. *The Brave*

Mori, Kyoko. *Shizuko's Daughter*

Morris, Winifred. *Liar*

Paulsen, Gary. *Harris & Me*

Rapp, Adam. *The Buffalo Tree*

Rottman, S. L. *Hero*

Womack, Jack. *Random Acts of Senseless Violence*

The Truth and Nothing But . . .

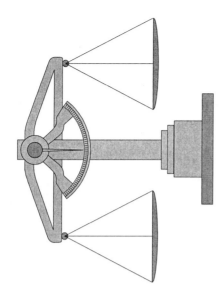

Avi. *Nothing but the Truth*

Bridger, Sue Ellen. *Keeping Christina*

Day, David. *The Walking Catfish*

Karr, Mary. *The Liar's Club: A Memoir*

Marino, Jan. *The Day That Elvis Came to Town*

Morris, Winifred. *Liar*

Peterson, P. J. *Liars*

Roos, Stephen. *Confessions of a Wayward Preppie*

Schwartz, Alvin. *Whoppers: Tall Tales and Other Lies*

Westall, Robert. *Yaxley's Cat*

Nixon, Joan Lowery
Don't Scream

LC 96-2436. 1996. 165p. $15.95 (ISBN 0-385-32065-5). Delacorte Press. 1996. 165p. $4.50pa. (ISBN 0-440-22710-0). Laurel-Leaf/ Bantam Doubleday Dell Books for Young Readers.

Genres: Contemporary realistic fiction, mystery

Themes: Crime, juvenile crime, family life, friendship, trust, fear, FBI, neighborhood, witness protection program, sociopaths, lying, volunteers, investigators, Internet, peer pressure, journalism, poison

Reading level: Fifth grade

Interest level: Eighth through twelfth grade

Reviews:
The Book Report. 15(4):37 January/February 1997.
School Library Journal. 42(11):124 November 1996.
Voice of Youth Advocates. 19(8):331–32 February 1997. (#3 quality, #3 popularity)

Author Information

Born in Los Angeles, Joan Lowery Nixon has moved around the West with her husband, who is a petroleum geologist. She graduated from the University of Southern California with a journalism degree but found herself teaching kindergarten and enjoyed that so much she went back to school to obtain a teacher's certificate. A prolific and popular author of children's and young adult books, Nixon has been writing since she was seventeen. She loves to write books with a hopeful message and likes to include some humor in her suspenseful books to break the tension. Nixon now lives in Houston, Texas, and continues to teach and write, drawing on her own memories of difficult teenage years. She is a charter member of the Society of Children's Book Writers and is a member and past officer of the Mystery Writers of America.

Plot Summary

Inquisitive Jess is intrigued by her charming new neighbor and classmate, Mark. At the same time, her best friend Lori has crossed paths with Scott, another new and attractive high school student. Handsome though they are, Scott's brooding secrecy and Mark's inconsistent behavior trouble Jess. With the help of her techie friend Eric, she investigates them both for a journalism assignment, and what she discovers puts her life in peril.

Introducing the Book

The rapid pace and easy reading of *Don't Scream* is typical of Nixon's popular mysteries. Once readers start, they will be anxious to find out just who the bad guy is, and that information is not revealed until the very end. To hook readers, read aloud chapter 1, skipping the "Confidential" file preceding page 7 (hardback and paperback editions).

Booktalks

On the Spot

Two cute new boys in school—what could be better? But one of them is evil. Which one? *Don't Scream* yet; read the book!

With the Author's Words

The Judge: "I've dealt with enough sociopaths to know they can be quite disarming and skilled at telling convincing lies . . . from the time [he] was nine until his last arrest at the age of fifteen, he compiled a long record of arrests for burglary, shoplifting, animal abuse, and—what worries me the most—brutality against other children." (p. 4, hardback and paperback editions)

A high school student's mother: "What a lovely boy . . . There's something different about him. He's so polite . . . so . . . I guess I'd say charming. That's it. He's charming." (p. 30, hardback and paperback editions)

He's brutal, he's charming, and he's in your school. *Don't Scream.*

Literature Extensions/Alternative Book Report Activities

Government/Witness Protection Program/Internet—Students will be intrigued by the witness protection program and Scott's ability to change his identity using the "Tombstone" method. Begin a study of witness protection and the Victim and Witness Protection Act of 1982 by searching the archives of the U.S. Department of Justice at http://www.usdoj.gov/ghindex.html and such Internet news sites as *Time*'s "Pathfinder" at http://pathfinder.com and *The New York Times* at http://www.nytimes.com. Challenge students to see if they can find anything specific on the "Tombstone" method.

Social Issues/Volunteering—Jess's idea about developing a volunteer program for a local hospital becomes a project for her social problems class. Volunteering can be a benefit for both students and the community. Students should be aware that volunteerism gives work experience (in addition to helping the community) and looks great on résumés and college applications. Consult *150 Ways Teens Can Make a Difference: A Handbook for Action* by Marian Salzman, et al. (Peterson's Guides, 1991); *Generation React: Activism for Beginners* by Danny Seo (Ballantine Books, 1997); and *It's Our World, Too! Stories of Young People Who Are Making a Difference* by Phillip Hoose (Joy Street, 1993).

Journalism/Investigative Reporting—Jess's journalism teacher tells students how to become good investigative reporters by using primary sources, interviews, the public library, city directories, civil and criminal court records, voter registration records, and the like (see pp. 76–82, hardback and paperback editions). Using these sources and others, students can select a subject, mount an investigation, and discover some secrets on their own.

Creative Writing/Headlines—One of the journalism class assignments was to create headlines for untitled newspaper articles. Provide students with a variety of articles from mainstream newspapers as well as tabloid journals. Depending on the tone of the article, have students write appropriate, attention-getting headlines.

Rip-Roaring Nixon Mysteries

Don't Scream (c1996)

Spirit Seeker (c1995)

Shadowmaker (c1994)

The Name of the Game Was Murder (c1993)

The Weekend Was Murder! (c1992)

A Candidate for Murder (c1991)

Whispers from the Dead (c1989)

The Dark and Deadly Pool (c1987)

The Ghosts of Now (c1984)

The Spector (c1982)

The Kidnapping of Christina Lattimore (c1979)

Who Done It? Mysteries

Goodman, Jonathan. Acts of Murder

Green, Kate. Black Dreams

Jones, Frank. Beyond Suspicion: True Stories of Unexpected Killers

Koontz, Dean R. Cold Fire

Koontz, Dean R. Mammoth Book of Murder

Michaels, Barbara. Houses of Stone

Nixon, Joan Lowery. Whispers of the Dead

Roberts, Nora. Entranced

Roberts, Nora. Solved; And, Unsolved: Classic True Murder Cases

West, Rosemary. Watcher in the Woods

Wynn, Douglas. Blind Justice: Ten Killers Who Almost Got Away with Murder

YA Mystery Writers

Jay Bennett

Caroline B. Cooney

Robert Cormier

Lois Duncan

Daniel Hayes

Joan Lowery Nixon

Willo Davis Roberts

Robert Westall

Patricia Windsor

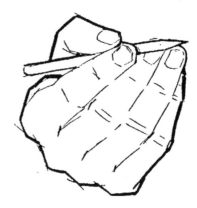

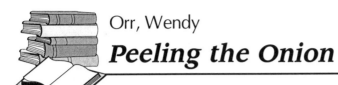

Orr, Wendy

Peeling the Onion

LC 96-42353. 1997. 166p. $15.95 (ISBN 0-8234-1289-X).
Holiday House.

Genres: Contemporary realistic fiction, romance, multicultural

Themes: Accidents, traffic accidents, pain, anger, grief, guilt, love, friendship, courage, spinal injuries, head trauma, hospitals, Australia, convalescence, family, karate, martial arts, sports, boy/girl relationships, disabilities, depression, humiliation, meditation, tutoring, euthanasia, physical therapy, suicide, counseling

Reading level: Sixth grade

Interest level: Eighth grade and up

Reviews:
Booklist. 93(15):1322 April 1, 1997.
Bulletin of the Center for Children's Books. 50(11):406 July/August 1997. (Recommended)
Publishers Weekly. 244(10):67 March 10, 1997.
School Library Journal. 43(5):138 May 1997. (Starred)
Voice of Youth Advocates. 20(4):246 October 1997. (#4 quality, #4 popularity)

Author Information

Wendy Orr has been writing books for children for years, but *Peeling the Onion* is her first book for young adults. Her own severe car accident six years ago provided the impetus for this story. Her life was permanently altered when she learned that total recovery was impossible. Writing Anna's story became a way for Orr to explore her own feelings. Orr was born in Canada and has lived in France and the United States. She now makes her home in Australia with her family, which consists of a husband, two kids, dogs, a cat, and cows. Visit "Wendy Orr's Bookweb" at http://www.cnl.com.au/users/wendyorr/.

Plot Summary

Seventeen-year-old Anna seems to have the world by the tail. She's a karate champion hoping to win awards and is about to begin her final year of high school. Then her life changes instantly after her involvement in a terrible car accident. Coping with constant pain (from multiple injuries—brain, spinal chord, thumb, ankle) and the eventual realization that her life is changed forever, Anna reacts with anger and grief. Bolstered by the support of her close-knit family, Anna's friendships and romances change as she slowly comes to grips with her new self.

Introducing the Book

Because teens often feel invulnerable, the drama of a teen becoming permanently disabled may be both chilling and fascinating. The short diary-like entries moving between the present and Anna's thoughts are appealing and make this a quick read. Consider reading aloud the first two chapters to entice readers and make them comfortable with the Australian terms that are defined in context.

Booktalks

On the Spot

Anna is in constant pain—physical pain, unbearable pain, and psychological pain. Her future dreams have been smashed, and her psyche is peeling away like an onion. What will be left of her?

With the Author's Words

A car crash happens with the speed of light. It happens to Anna and this is her memory.

> *A Star of shattered glass, cold against my temple.*
> *Blackness.*
> *Sinking in the woolly blackness, choking, drowning, suffocating.*

I want to claw my way out but can't move, want to scream but don't know how. The blackness is swallowing me and I know that if I can't fight it the me will be gone and the blackness will go on without end. (p. 1, hardback edition)

This is fear. This is pain. This is *Peeling the Onion*.

Literature Extensions/Alternative Book Report Activities

Biology/Brain Research—New technologies for studying genes and new and powerful brain scanning equipment have allowed scientists to obtain a much clearer picture of the brain's inner workings. Expose students to new research about brain development, including information about the brain's ability to construct new pathway connections.

Although most in-depth scientific information isn't explored in the popular press, this particular topic was featured in major news stories or special publications by national magazines and newspapers. Consult *Newsweek*'s "Special Issue: Your Child from Birth to Three" (Spring/Summer 1997, pp. 28–39); *Time* 149(5):48–61 February 3, 1997; and *Newsweek* 127(8):54–62 February 19, 1996. Discuss the importance of this research, why the popular press highlighted it, and the implications for education and child care.

Creative Writing/Poetry/Metaphors/Internet—To satisfy an English assignment, Anna uses an onion as a metaphor in a poem to express how she feels about herself. At different stages, she goes back and rewrites her first attempt of "Peeling the Onion." (pp. 92–93, 120, and 166, hardback edition)

Students often have difficulty understanding literary devices such as metaphor. This concrete example plus those exemplified in the following picture books for older readers will help: *Switch on the Night* by Ray Bradbury (Alfred A. Knopf, 1993); *An Actor* (1987), *An Artist* (1980), *School of Names* (1986), and *A Writer* (1984), all by M. B Goffstein and published by Harper & Row; *An Angel for Solomon Singer* by Cynthia Rylant (Orchard Books, 1992); and *The Wretched Stone* by Chris Van Allsburg (Houghton Mifflin, 1985).

In addition, there are some "survivor guilt" poetry sites that are quite moving and are a perfect fit with the "Peeling the Onion" poem. An example can be found at http://www.lib.uchicago.edu/~rd13/hd/guilt.html.

Current Events/Euthanasia/Debate—During the time when Anna's pain never ceases and she begins to realize that full recovery is impossible, she becomes aware of the public debate regarding euthanasia. "You can't open a paper or turn on the TV without hearing about euthanasia. The whole world's obsessed with it. And everyone's so adamant, whichever side they're on!" (p. 66, hardback edition) Use *Peeling the Onion* and this statement to launch a classic debate with students prepared by research to argue both sides of this topical issue.

Psychology/Survivor Guilt/Internet—War, accidents, transmitted diseases (such as AIDS), and disasters (e.g., transportation crashes, earthquakes, and floods) produce a special form of remorse in those who survive. After the car accident, Hayden suffers this "survivor guilt," displayed by his exaggerated sense of responsibility for Anna.

Exploration of the Internet via search engines and directories will acquaint students with information about survivors who experience dreams and nightmares. Some sites provide information about coping techniques, such as visualization, writing poems, and the like. Working in groups, students can find the currently relevant Internet sites and research different aspects of this psychological disorder.

Australian Authors Young Adults Shouldn't Miss—

Graeme Base

Jill Ker Conway

Gary Crew

Mem Fox

Libby Hathorn

Paul Jennings

John Marsden

James Moloney

Garth Nix

Wendy Orr

Gillian Rubinstein

Colin Thiele

Nadia Wheatley

Patricia Wrightson

Courage: Beating the Odds

Bode, Janet. *Beating the Odds: Stories of Unexpected Achievers*

Calvert, Patricia. *Picking Up the Pieces*

Cheney, Glenn Alan. *Teens with Physical Disabilities*

Drimmer, Frederick. *Incredible People: Five Stories of Extraordinary Lives*

Hesse, Karen. *Out of the Dust*

Ingold, Jeanette. *The Window*

Johnston, Julie. *A Hero of a Lesser Cause*

Orr, Wendy. *Peeling the Onion*

Philbrick, Rodman. *Freak the Mighty*

Randle, Kristen D. *The Only Alien on the Planet*

Voigt, Cynthia. *Izzy, Willy-Nilly*

Wolff, Virginia Euwer. *Probably Still Nick Swansen: A Novel*

CRASH

Bennett, Jay. *Coverup*

Buffie, Margaret. *The Dark Garden*

Bunting, Eve. *A Sudden Silence*

Cooney, Caroline B. *Driver's Ed*

Draper, Sharon. *Tears of a Tiger*

Duncan, Lois. *I Know What You Did Last Summer*

Grant, Cynthia D. *Shadow Man*

McDaniel, Lurlene. *Somewhere Between Life and Death*

Orr, Wendy. *Peeling the Onion*

Stine, R. L. *Hit and Run*

Strasser, Todd. *The Accident*

Voigt, Cynthia. *Izzy, Willy-Nilly*

Snedden, Robert

Yuck! A Big Book of Little Horrors

LC 92-42364. 1996. unpaged. $15.00 (ISBN 0-689-80676-0). Simon & Schuster.

Genres: Nonfiction, humor

Themes: Microscopes, microbiology, bacteria, germs, fungi, photography, images, magnification, botany, insects, parasites

Reading level: Sixth grade

Interest level: Fifth grade and up

Reviews:
Booklist. 92(19/20):1714 June 1/15, 1996.
Bulletin of the Center for Children's Books.
49(10):353 June 1996. (Recommended)
Publishers Weekly. 243(20):76 May 13, 1996.
School Library Journal. 42(5):127 May 1996.

Author Information

Robert Snedden edited books for adults and children for more than thirteen years before he decided to become a freelance author on his own. He now writes nonfiction books for students, including a recent series of companion books, "What Is a . . .?"—about fish, mammals, birds, and so forth. Currently living in Twickenham, just outside London, Snedden was born in Scotland.

Plot Summary

Enlarged color photographs zero in on many of the tiny, gross common creatures that inhabit our world—our homes, our bodies, our food, and so on. The double-page spreads feature a "mystery" microscopic photograph on the left, and the answer, enhanced by more photographs and text, beneath the flap on the right. The book is guaranteed to give you the shivers! A companion to *Yuck!* is *Yikes* by Mike Janulewicz (Simon & Schuster, 1997).

Introducing the Book

Choose a couple of the enhanced photographs to show the class and ask students to identify the creature or object. After revealing the correct answer, be prepared for the book to be snatched away.

Booktalks

On the Spot

(Show the first photograph—"Hi mom, I'm home.") Is this creature *really* in your house? Or worse: Is it *on* you? To find out for sure—experience *Yuck!*

With the Author's Words

In the dark places of your home there is always something lurking. Scurrying here and there, they feel their way with long antennae that twitch constantly. They like the kitchen best because there are many dim, damp corners to hide in and there is plenty to eat. If you go into the kitchen tonight and turn the light on quickly you might just catch a few of your uninvited guests. If you're brave enough, that is, to come face to face with. . . . ("With the darkness comes" page)

(Show the blue monster featured in the photograph opposite the text above.)

Literature Extensions/Alternative Book Report Activities

Art/Bookmaking/Toy Books—*Yuck!* is a flap book, a "toy book" design that produces a particular effect. Other good flap book examples include John S. Goodall's series about England from medieval times to the present: *The Story of a Castle* (Atheneum, 1986); *The Story of a Farm* (Atheneum, 1989); *The Story of an English Village* (Atheneum, 1978); *The Story of a Main Street* (Atheneum, 1987); and *The Story of the Seashore* (Margaret K. McElderry Books, 1990). Provide these as models for students to use in bookmaking projects.

Biology/Microscopic Images/Internet—Even though most schools do not have equipment to see bacteria and other microscopic images magnified hundreds or thousands of times, students can view these images via Internet sites. Begin an exploration featuring images and links at the Boston Museum of Science's "Scanning Electron Microscope" at http://www.mos.org/sln/sem/. Continue by viewing a "Picture Gallery" at http://www-micrbiol.sci.kun.nl/micrbiol/micrgala.html, bacteria dividing and multiplying at http://www-micro.msb.le.ac.uk/Video/pneumo.html, and the "Dust Bunnies" that cause allergies at http://www.cellsalive.com/mite.htm.

Biology/Microorganisms—A study of microorganisms could be enhanced by the use of some of the following books: *Microorganisms: The Unseen World* by Edward R. Ricciuti (Blackbirch Marketing, 1994); *Mysterious Microbes* by Steve Parker (Raintree/Steck-Vaughn, 1994); *Cells, Genes, and Chromosomes* by Nuria Bosch Roca (Chelsea House, 1995); and *Guide to Microlife* by Kenneth G. Rainis and Bruce J. Russell (Franklin Watts, 1997). Exciting and entertaining projects in microbiology that teach analytical thought and scientific method are available in *Microbiology: High School Science Fair Experiments* by H. Steven Dashefsky (McGraw-Hill, 1994).

Vocational Education/Microscopes/Building/Internet—Vocational education students could make either of the following microscopes for classroom use in their school district. Instructions for making a standard microscope (http://www.mos.org/sln/sem/myomicro.html) and a stereoscopic microscope (http://www.best.com/~funsci/texts/uster1.htm) are available via these Internet sites.

Picture This: Real Science—Real Pictures

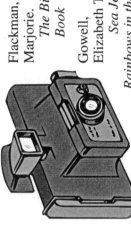

Flackman, Marjorie. *The Big Bug Book*

Gowell, Elizabeth T. *Sea Jellies: Rainbows in the Sea*

Janulewicz, Mike. *Yikes! Your Body, Up Close*

Kitchen, Bert. *And So They Build*

Kitchen, Bert. *Animal Alphabet*

Lauber, Patricia. *Seeing Earth from Space*

Lucht, Irmgard. *The Red Poppy*

Robbins, Ken. *A Flower Grows*

Simon, Seymour. *Our Solar System*

Snedden, Robert. *Yuck! A Big Book of Little Horrors*

Wexo, John Bonnett. *Animal Champions*

Books That =Move POP and Fold

Drescher, Henrik. *Pat the Beastie: A Pull-and-Poke Book*

Hewetson, Sarah. *Eye Magic: Fantastic Optical Illusions—An Interactive Pop-Up Book*

Hildebrandt, Greg. *Greg Hildebrandt's Book of Three-Dimensional Dragons*

N. E. Thing Enterprises. "Magic Eye" Books

Pelham, David. *Sam's Pizza: Your Pizza to Go*

Pelham, David. *Sam's Sandwich*

Pelham, David. *Sam's Snack*

Pienkowski, Jan. *Toilet Book*

Snedden, Robert. *Yuck! A Big Book of Little Horrors*

Sturgis, Alexander. *Optical Illusions in Art*

YUCK! and More Yuck

Aylesworth, Jim. *Old Black Fly*

Branzei, Sylvia. *Animal Grossology: The Science of Creatures Gross and Disgusting*

Branzei, Sylvia. *Grossology*

Cobb, Vicki. *For Your Own Protection*

Colombo, Luann. *Gross but True Creatures*

Colombo, Luann. *Gross but True Germs*

Drescher, Henrik. *Pat the Beastie: A Pull-and-Poke Book*

Elfman, Eric. *Almanac of the Gross, Disgusting & Totally Repulsive*

Janulewicz, Mike. *Yikes! Your Body, Up Close*

Lovett, Sarah. *Extremely Weird Micro Monsters*

Snedden, Robert. *Yuck! A Big Book of Little Horrors*

Plummer, Louise

The Unlikely Romance of Kate Bjorkman

LC 94-49614. 1995. 183p. $15.95 (ISBN 0-385-32049-3). Delacorte Press. 1997. 192p. $4.95pa. (ISBN 0-440-22704-6). Laureleaf Books/Bantam Doubleday Dell.

Genres: Contemporary realistic fiction, humor, romance

Themes: Writing, family life, love, romance, truth, friendship, jealousy, linguistics, boy/girl relationships, brothers and sisters, betrayal, forgiveness, Christmas, ice skating

Reading level: Sixth grade

Interest level: Eighth through twelfth grade

Reviews:
> *The Book Report.* 14(4):47 January/February 1996.
> *Bulletin of the Center for Children's Books.* 49(3):103 November 1995.
> *Horn Book.* 72(2):213 March/April 1996.
> *Publishers Weekly.* 242(43):70 October 23, 1995.
> *School Library Journal.* 41(10):160 October 1995. (Starred review)

Author Information

A Salt Lake City, Utah, resident, Louise Plummer was born in the Netherlands and immigrated to the United States with her parents when she was five years old. Her master's degree in English is from the University of Minnesota, and she currently teaches writing at Brigham Young University.

Plot Summary

Seventeen-year-old Kate Bjorkman is writing a romance novel, but it won't include three-paragraph kisses, a hero with a masculine name, and a virginal heroine with long, silky legs. What it does feature is an honest accounting of Kate's Christmas romance with her brother's best friend, vivid descriptions of her solid family and her traitorous best friend, and the agonies and ecstasies of falling in love.

Introducing the Book

Any reader looking for a funny, light, tongue-in-cheek romance will snap this one up. This fast-paced novel of teen romance and an unlikely heroine is not typical of the genre. To introduce readers to the intriguing style, read the short prologue aloud.

Booktalks

On the Spot

Will tall and handsome Richard dump the tall and nearly blind Kate for the sexy Ashley? Will Kate ever find true love? Some may say it's *The Unlikely Romance of Kate Bjorkman.*

With the Author's Words

> *"Hi," I said and stepped forward to shake hands, when I tripped on the edge of the oriental carpet and lurched into him, elbows first. It wasn't a pretty picture. He made a sound like 'oomph' because my elbow caught him in the diaphragm. He was too incapacitated for me to fall gracefully into his arms. Instead, I was caught by a drop-dead-beautiful young woman standing at Richard's shoulder. This would be a better story if I'd just lie, but I want truth in romance. And the truth is that the first time I saw Richard Bradshaw after four years of separation, I knocked the wind out of him and was saved from falling on my face by his girlfriend. (pp. 13–14, paperback and hardback editions)*

Meet Kate Bjorkman—klutzy, six feet tall, Coke-bottle glasses, and trying to find romance. Unlikely?

Literature Extensions/Alternative Book Report Activities

Creative Writing/Magazines/Publications/Internet—Louise Plummer's character Kate writes this first-person narrative of romance for potential publication. Teen writing is regularly published in a variety of forms, such as short stories, poetry, essays, and so on. The annual magazine *Merlyn's Pen: Fiction, Essays and Poems by America's Teens* is a great example of published teen writing. This company also publishes The American Teen Writer Series, anthologies that include works previously published in the annual magazines. Visit their Website at http://www.merlynspen.com and encourage students to submit work.

Writers in your class can also visit the following Internet sites for young authors. Notice that many of them provide opportunities for submission: "Young Authors Workshop" at http://www.planet.eon.net/~bplaroch/Publish.html; "For Young Writers" (advice from published children's authors, editors, and publishers) at http://www.inkspot.com/youngadvice.html; and "Writes of Passage" at http://www.writes.org/index.htm.

Creative Writing/References—Kate often refers to *The Romance Writer's Phrase Book*, a tool she uses to guide her romantic writing. Burgeoning writers will be glad to know about the variety of writer's guides available that feature words, phrases, and writing styles for all sorts of genres. Provide some of these, such as *The New Comprehensive American Rhyming Dictionary* by Sue Young (William Morrow and Company, 1991); *Contemporary American Slang* by Richard A. Spears (National Textbook Company, 1991); *Whistlin' Dixie: A Dictionary of Southern Expressions* by Robert Hendrickson (Facts on File, 1993); *Dictionary of the American West* by Winfred Blevins (Facts on File, 1993); *Writing Crime Fiction* by H. R. F. Keating (St. Martin's Press, 1986); and *How to Write Horror Fiction* by William F. Nolan (Writer's Digest Books, 1990).

Health/Psychology/Relationships/Communication—When Kate's brother and his new wife have an argument, one of the house guests comments, "they need to talk about how they're going to make decisions when they don't agree." (p. 88, paperback and hardback editions) This fundamental truth applies to every relationship. Recent publications concerning male and female communication point out the need to learn how to communicate more effectively. Provide students with such books as *Sex Ed: Growing Up, Relationships, and Sex* by Miriam Stoppard (Dorling Kindersley, 1997); *Friendshifts: The Power of Friendship and How It Shapes Our Lives* by Jan Yager (Hannacroix Creek Books, 1997); *Anybody Got a Clue About Guys? A Young Woman's Guide to Healthy Relationships* by Susie Shellenberger (Vine Books, 1995); *Love Needs Learning: A Relationship Course for Young People* by Margaret Vincent (Geoffrey Chapman, 1994); and *Mars and Venus on a Date: A Guide for Navigating the 5 Stages of Dating to Create a Loving and Lasting Relationship* by John Gray (HarperCollins, 1997).

Language/Linguistics—Kate's father is a professor of linguistics, and she has an avid interest in that field as well. If possible, invite a linguist to your class to demonstrate his or her skill in determining where a person was raised based on their accent. Applicable books include *ABC's of Languages and Linguistics: A Practical Primer to Language Science* by Curtis W. Hayes, et al. (National Textbook Company, 1989); *American in So Many Words: Words That Have Shaped America* by David K. Barnhart and Allan A. Metcalf (Houghton Mifflin, 1997); *An Index by Region, Usage, and Etymology of American Regional English* by Allan A. Metcalf and Luanne Von Schneidemesser (University of Alabama Press, 1993); *Aw, Shucks! The Dictionary of Country Jawing* by Anne Bertram (National Textbook Company, 1996); and *Broadcast Voice Handbook: How to Polish Your On-Air Delivery* by Ann S. Utterback (Bonus Books, 1995).

Teen Writers

Allen, R. E. *Ozzy on the Outside*

Crutcher, Chris. *Ironman*

Cushman, Karen. *Catherine, Called Birdy*

Davis, Terry. *If Rock and Roll Were a Machine*

Deem, James M. *The 3 NBs of Julian Drew*

Plummer, Louise. *The Unlikely Romance of Kate Bjorkman*

Rottman, S. L. *Hero*

Thomas, Rob. *Rats Saw God*

Trembath, Don. *A Fly Named Alfred*

Trembath, Don. *The Tuesday Cafe*

Christmas Tales for Teens

Breathed, Berkeley. *Red Ranger Came Calling: A Guaranteed True Christmas Story*

Bunting, Eve. *December*

Collington, Peter. *A Small Miracle*

Cooney, Caroline B. *What Child Is This?*

Day, Alexandra, and Cooper Edens. *The Christmas We Moved to the Barn*

Henry, O. *The Gift of the Magi and Other Stories*. Illus. by Michael Dooling

Jukes, Mavis. *Lights Around the Palm*

McKissack, Patricia C., and Fredrick L. McKissack. *Christmas in the Big House, Christmas in the Quarters*

Moser, Barry. *Good and Perfect Gifts: A Retelling of O. Henry's The Gift of the Magi*

Nettell, Stephanie. *A Christmas Treasury*

Plummer, Louise. *The Unlikely Romance of Kate Bjorkman*

Willard, Nancy. *Cracked Corn and Snow Ice Cream*

Romantic Comedies

Clements, Bruce. *Tom Loves Anna Loves Tom*

Daly, Maureen. *Act of Love*

Herrick, Ann. *The Perfect Guy*

Kaplow, Peter. *Alessandra in Love*

Kaplow, Peter. *Alessandra in Between*

Plummer, Louise. *My Name Is Sus5an Smith, The 5 Is Silent*

Plummer, Louise. *The Unlikely Romance of Kate Bjorkman*

Sheldon, Dyan. *The Boy of My Dreams*

Wersba, Barbara. *Love Is the Crooked Thing*

Sleator, William
The Night the Heads Came

LC 95-32321. 1996. 154p. $15.99 (ISBN 0-525-45463-2). Dutton.

Genres: Science fiction, mystery, adventure

Themes: Aliens, abduction, extraterrestrials, kidnapping, time, space travel, artists, drawing, dimensions, environment, sabotage, evil, spacecraft, hypnosis, false memories, pollution, revenge, hypnotism, emotions

Reading level: Fifth grade

Interest level: Sixth through twelfth grade

Reviews:
The Book Report. 15(2):43 September/October 1996.
Booklist. 92(14):1252 March 15, 1996. (Boxed review)
Bulletin of the Center for Children's Books. 49(7):243 March 1996.
Publishers Weekly. 243(8):217 February 19, 1996.
School Library Journal. 42(4):158 April 1996.

Author Information

Fascinated by music as well as things "grotesque and macabre," William Sleator studied music at Harvard (which he hated) and preserved his sanity by writing constantly in his journals. A pianist for England's Royal Ballet School after college, Sleator eventually toured for nine years with the Boston Ballet and traveled throughout Europe. Now he does what he loves best—writing science fiction. He enjoys writing about fantasy and magic and about things that might really be possible. According to the biographical information on the flyleaf of *The Night the Heads Came*, "They" will come back for Sleator only if he writes and publishes this book. So now . . . he's waiting. Find out more about Sleator and the family he grew up with in his autobiographical book entitled *Oddballs* (Dutton, 1993).

Plot Summary

Sixteen-year-olds Leo and Tim are abducted by aliens on a lonely country road in New York, but only Leo returns, and no one believes his story. A psychologist nearly convinces Leo that his experiences are too silly to be true, but when Tim shows up two days later and two years older, Leo knows that he must uncover the truth of the abduction. What follows is a tangle of environmental sabotage, evil, and alien involvement.

Introducing the Book

Fans of *The X-Files* will love this accounting of abduction, lost time, implants, and conspiracy. Talk about the alien theories revealed in the popular television series, read aloud the first chapter of *The Night the Heads Came* or the author's comments on the back flyleaf, and observe the abduction of this book!

Booktalks

On the Spot

Two days after he is abducted by aliens, sixteen-year-old Tim returns with bizarre three-dimensional drawings of alien worlds. Stranger still, Tim has aged two years, and he's in terrible danger.

With the Author's Words

It's the ideal time and place for an abduction—late at night on a lonely country road . . . and Leo's car stops without explanation.

> *I squirm around in the seat to press the lock on the door behind me. But I can't find it. Because the door behind me is already open. I feel the warm air blowing in. And then a delicate touch on the back of my neck, rough and moist and cold, like an animal's tongue . . . I scream; I can't help it. Tim screams too. And when we stop screaming we hear the high-pitched, soft chittering sounds coming from the backseat. And something laps my neck again. (p. 6, hardback edition)*

That's no animal's tongue . . . And those chittering noises? They belong to the aliens who soon take Leo and Tim aboard their scary, grimy spacecraft. It's a night no one will forget. It's *The Night the Heads Came*.

Literature Extensions/Alternative Book Report Activities

Art/Drawing/Careers/Internet—Tim is returned to Earth two days after being abducted by aliens and has brought back bizarre three-dimensional drawings of alien worlds. Regardless of the truth of Tim's experiences, the three-dimensional drawings are extremely interesting. Learning to draw (and think) in perspective is important to budding artists and computer graphic designers. Introduce students to sketching, instruments, and computer-assisted design software used in producing perspective drawings.

The following Websites have lesson plans to help students with drawing in perspective: "Drawing: Perspective, Shading and Composition" at http://www.saumag.edu/art/studio/chalkboard/draw.html and "Perspective Drawing" at http://forum.swarthmore.edu/sum95/math_and/perspective/perspect.html, which also includes a discussion about perspective and selected links to pictures in perspective on the Web.

Science/Environment/Community Action—The alien Others warn Earth inhabitants that the destruction of their planet is unavoidable unless they change their ways. Sleator's book provides an easy segue to further discussion and exploration concerning the environment. Some schools have a "Green" group that organizes recycling; others provide time for students to participate in community projects that emphasize kindness to the Earth. Collect a series of Internet Websites, books, pamphlets, and periodical articles with information on this topic and help students become actively involved with the environment for their future.

UFOs/Extraterrestrial Life—Are there UFOs? Have extraterrestrials visited Earth? These questions have been pondered and explored by many people for years. Hollywood productions that feature alien abductions, UFOs, and extraterrestrials continue to keep this subject alive and well. It will be a popular topic of research for students. Challenge them to seek further information with comprehensive books such as *The UFO Book: Encyclopedia of the Extraterrestrial* by Jerome Clark (Visible Ink Press, 1997) and *Fifty Years of UFOs: From Distant Sightings to Close Encounters* by John Spencer and Anne Spencer (Boxtree, 1997).

Psychology/Hypnotism/False Memories/Current Events—A psychologist nearly convinces Leo that his experience with alien abduction is too silly to be true, but when Tim shows up two days later (and two years older), Leo knows that he must uncover the truth. Although this is fiction, the psychological issue of "false memories" is an interesting and contemporary topic for research and debate.

In 1997, Elizabeth Loftus, University of Washington, reported research suggesting that at least 25 percent of the population is susceptible to having false memories planted in their brains. The researchers used methods similar to those which therapists use to retrieve repressed memories from victims of suspected abuse.

What can your students discover about false memories and the debate that continues in the psychology profession and popular press? Helpful books include *Diagnosis for Disaster: The Devastating Truth About False Memory Syndrome and Its Impact on Accusers and Families* by Claudette Wassil-Grimm (Penguin, 1996); *Memory Quest: Trauma and the Search for Personal History* by Elizabeth A. Waites (W. W. Norton, 1997); and *The Recovered Memory/False Memory Debate,* edited by Kathy Pezdek and William P. Banks (Academic Press, 1996).

Ghostly Appearances & Shape Changers

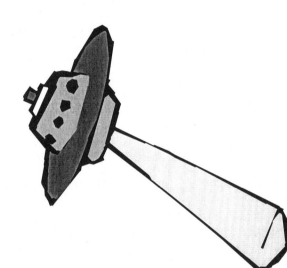

Buffie, Margaret. *The Dark Garden*

Carr, A. A. *Eye Killers*

Hahn, Mary Downing. *Look for Me by Moonlight*

Kindl, Patrice. *Owl in Love*

Klause, Annette Curtis. *Blood and Chocolate*

Klause, Annette Curtis. *The Silver Kiss*

Mahy, Margaret. *The Changeover: A Supernatural Romance*

Morrison, Toni. *Beloved*

Preiss, Byron, and John Betancourt, eds. *The Ultimate Zombie*

Rubinstein, Gillian. *Galax-Arena*

Saberhagen, Fred. *Dancing Bears*

Sleator, William. *Dangerous Wishes*

Sleator, William. *The Night the Heads Came*

Velde, Vivian Vande. *Companions of the Night*

The Truth Is Out There: Aliens & UFOs

Clute, John. *Science Fiction: The Illustrated Encyclopedia*

Dexter, Catherine. *Alien Game*

Marsh, Carole E. *Unidentified Flying Objects and Extraterrestrial Life*

Preiss, Byron, and John Betancourt, eds. *The Ultimate Alien*

Schusterman, Neal. *The Dark Side of Nowhere: A Novel*

Sleator, William. *The Night the Heads Came*

Save the Earth—Novels

Brown, Paul. *Greenpeace*

Cardillo, Joe. *Pulse*

DeFelice, Cynthia. *Lostman's River*

Hesse, Karen. *Phoenix Rising*

Klass, David. *California Blue*

Lipsyte, Robert. *Chemo Kid*

Sleator, William. *The Night the Heads Came*

Thompson, Julian. *Gypsy World*

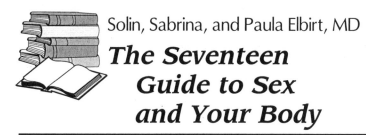

Solin, Sabrina, and Paula Elbirt, MD

The Seventeen Guide to Sex and Your Body

LC 96-16230. 1996. 130p. $17.00 (ISBN 0-689-90796-1). Aladdin. 1996. $8.99pa. (ISBN 0-689-80795-3). Aladdin.

Genre: Nonfiction

Themes: Adolescent development, sexuality, health, puberty, hygiene, physical development, questions and answers

Reading level: Upper fifth grade

Interest level: Seventh grade and up

Reviews:
Booklist. 93(3):332 October 1, 1996.

Bulletin of the Center for Children's Books. 50(5):185–86 January 1997.
Kliatt Paperback and Audio Book Guide. 31(1):22 January 1997.
Publishers Weekly. 243(32):443 August 5, 1996.
School Library Journal. 42(11):130 November 1996.
Voice of Youth Advocates. 20(2):138 June 1997. (#4 quality, #4 popularity)

Author Information

Sabrina Solin edits the "Sex and Body" column of *Seventeen* magazine. Every month she gets hundreds of letters from teens who are concerned about their changing bodies. Often they wonder if their experiences are weird or normal, and many of the letters ask the same questions. In an effort to let girls know what to expect as their bodies change and to serve as a comfort as they go through these changes, Dr. Paula Elbirt (a medical expert) and Solin wrote *The Seventeen Guide to Sex and Your Body*.

Plot Summary

This self-help guide uses a question-and-answer format with actual questions gleaned from *Seventeen* magazine's "Sex and Body" column. Clear information and honest answers respond to queries that range from physical development to birth control to dating to sexually transmitted diseases to rape. The style is conversational, and the informational is topical.

Introducing the Book

Teen girls *and* boys are interested in materials covering the bumpy journey through puberty, but some may be reluctant to ask for related books. Using the bookmarks below, create a materials collection to generate knowledge, self-respect, and responsibility.

Booktalks

On the Spot

Ever worry about what's going on with your body? Or—exactly what to do on a date? You're not alone—the questions are asked *and* answered in *The Seventeen Guide to Sex and Your Body*.

With the Author's Words

Most girls want to know if what they're going through is normal (usually it is, even if it feels weird). And of course, a lot of you have questions about guys . . . and sex. It's freaky enough to have your body transform before your eyes, but at the same time, you're dealing with a lot of stuff that can make you feel pretty clueless. (introduction)

Feel clueless no longer after discovering that *everyone* wants to know what you want to know. It's all in *The Seventeen Guide to Sex and Your Body*.

Literature Extensions/Alternative Book Report Activities

Classroom Collection—Episodic reading is perfect for reluctant readers, and magazines are perfect for episodic reading. Develop a classroom collection of magazines geared for teenagers. According to many librarians on the PUBYAC (public young adult and children's librarians) listserv, current popular titles include *Seventeen*, *Nintendo Power*, *Mad Magazine*, *Electronic Gaming Monthly*, *Teen Beat*, *YM*, *Teen*, *Transworld Skateboarding*, *Vibe*, *Rolling Stone*, *Wizard*, *GamePlayer*, *GamePro*, *Source*, *Rap Pages*, and *Sports Illustrated*. However, because magazine publications come and go, ask your students to suggest their current favorites.

Health/Resources/Internet—There are a variety of agencies and organizations that specialize in assisting teens. Develop a collection of pamphlets, bookmarks, and handouts that will guide teenagers to appropriate local support groups. Use the bookmarks to acquaint your students with your collection and assemble a listing of the toll-free numbers for national support organizations. Bookmark Internet sites of interest on your computer or develop a section on your home page with links to helpful agencies.

Health/Sex Education/Research—Students can select one or more of any of the topics mentioned in *The Seventeen Guide to Sex and Your Body* for further research. They can find out the latest information on toxic shock syndrome, PMS, breast cancer, or food myths and facts. Point them toward traditional research sources as well as local health care clinics.

Writing/Newspapers/Research—Discovering information via advice columns is a popular activity for all ages. If your school newspaper does not have an advice column, consider creating one. Some community newspapers regularly feature articles from high school newspapers. Perhaps your local paper will print a regular "Teen to Teen" advice column?

Students who wish to provide answers or counseling must agree to conduct appropriate research, including contacting professionals and experts when necessary.

Health—The Basics

Abner, Allison, and Linda Villarosa. *Finding Our Way: The Teen Girls' Survival Guide*

Bell, Ruth. *Changing Bodies, Changing Lives*

Cornog, Martha, and Timothy Perper. *For Sex Education, See Librarian: A Guide to Issues and Resources*

Harris, Robie H. *It's Perfectly Normal: Changing Bodies, Growing Up, Sex, and Sexual Health*

Isler, Charlotte, and Alwyn T. Cohall. *The Watts Teen Health Dictionary*

Jukes, Mavis. *It's a Girl Thing: How to Stay Healthy, Safe, and in Charge*

McCoy, Kathy. *The New Teenage Body Book*

Nottridge, Rhoda. *Care for Your Body*

Solin, Sabrina. *The Seventeen Guide to Sex and Your Body*

Weston, Carol. *Girltalk: All the Stuff Your Sister Never Told You*

Sex—What About It?

Akagi, Cynthia. *Dear Larissa: Sexuality Education for Girls Ages 11–17*

Akagi, Cynthia. *Dear Michael: Sexuality Education for Boys Ages 11–17*

Fenwick, Elizabeth. *How Sex Works*

Ferguson, Robert. *A Guide to Rape Awareness and Prevention*

Hicks, John. *Dating Violence: True Stories of Hurt and Hope*

Nardo, Don. *Teen Sexuality*

Roberts, Tara, ed. *Am I the Last Virgin? Ten African-American Reflections on Sex and Love*

Short, Ray. *Sex, Dating and Love*

Solin, Sabrina. *The Seventeen Guide to Sex and Your Body*

Sutton, Roger. *Hearing Us Out: Voices from the Gay and Lesbian Community*

Wirths, Claudine. *Choosing Is Confusing: How to Make Good Choices, Not Bad Guesses*

Fighting the Food Fight—Eating Disorders

Bode, Janet. *Food Fight: A Guide to Eating Disorders for Pre-Teens and Their Parents*

Cassell, Dana. *Encyclopedia of Obesity and Eating Disorders*

Dawson, Jill. *How Do I Look?*

Folkers, Gladys, and Jeanne Engelmann. *Taking Charge of My Mind and Body: A Girl's Guide to Outsmarting Alcohol, Drugs, Smoking, and Eating Disorders*

Hipp, Earl. *Feed Your Head: Some Excellent Stuff on Being Yourself*

Kolodny, Nancy J. *When Food's a Foe: How to Confront and Conquer Eating Disorders*

Landau, Elaine. *Weight: A Teenage Concern*

Moe, Barbara. *Coping with Eating Disorders*

Newman, Leslie. *Fat Chance*

Ojeda, Linda. *Safe Dieting for Teens*

Solin, Sabrina. *The Seventeen Guide to Sex and Your Body*

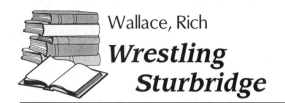 Wallace, Rich

Wrestling Sturbridge

LC 95-20468. 1996. 133p. $16.00 (ISBN 0-679-87803-3). Alfred A. Knopf. 1996. 135p. $4.99pa. (ISBN 0-679-88555-2). Alfred A. Knopf. 3 cassettes, 3.25 hours. Read by Johnny Heller. 1996. $26.00. Recorded Books. Plot notes.

Genres: Contemporary realistic fiction, sports, romance, multicultural

Themes: Wrestling, determination, coming-of-age, competition, friendship, high school life, boy/girl relationships, religion, secrets, small-town life, anger, fair play, factories, fear, stealing, racism, hunting

Reading level: Fifth grade

Interest level: Eighth through twelfth grade

Reviews:

The Book Report. 15(3):44 November/December 1996.

Booklist. 93(1):128 September 1, 1996. (Starred review)

Horn Book. 72(6):747 November/December 1996.

Kliatt Paperback and Audio Book Guide. 31(5):15 September 1997.

Publishers Weekly. 243(23):84 June 3, 1996.

School Library Journal. 42(10):150 October 1996.

Voice of Youth Advocates. 20(2):114 June 1997. (#5 quality, #4 popularity)

Author Information

Rich Wallace has loved sports as long as he can remember. In college, he says he preferred track and field over all else. Today Wallace coaches several youth sports teams and runs daily. As an adolescent, Wallace kept intricate journals that he now uses as source material to reflect the tumultuous teenage years. At work on a new novel, Wallace juggles homelife with his work as coordinating editor at *Highlights for Children*. He writes when his wife (a nurse on the late shift) is at work. Interestingly enough, Wallace was never a wrestler.

Plot Summary

In small-town Sturbridge, Pennsylvania, being a wrestling champ is all-important. As a senior varsity wrestler, Ben hopes to win the state championship in his weight class. Unfortunately, he is in the same weight category as Al, "the first-best 135-pound wrestler in the state" (flyleaf, hardback edition), and Al is one of Ben's best friends. Ben wrestles with his thoughts as he wonders if he should challenge Al, or declare Kim Chavez his girlfriend, or just knuckle down and write his college application. Graduation is just around the corner, and Ben has no intention of staying in Sturbridge.

Introducing the Book

To introduce the book to potential readers (including non-sports fans), select and read aloud some of Ben's "Best and Worst" lists placed between many of the twenty-two chapters. High school juniors and seniors will identify with many of Ben's agonies of indecision.

Booktalks

On the Spot

If winning the state wrestling championship means beating out one of your best friends, would you do it? No? Even if it's the most important thing in the world to you?

With the Author's Words

Al is scared. He may be the best high school wrestler in this state—everybody who knows him seems to think so. I think so, too. But there's one guy left who can take him. One guy who really believes he can do it. And that guy used to be Al's best friend. (p. 114, hardback edition)

That guy is Ben—and his story is *Wrestling Sturbridge*.

Literature Extensions/Alternative Book Report Activities

Careers/Colleges/Internet—Ben has procrastinated about applying to colleges, and graduation is looming ahead. Students who plan to attend college should be planning throughout their high school years. Provide a variety of guides for students to use, such as *College Planning for Dummies* by Pat Ordovensky (IDG Books, 1997); *The College Application Essay* by Sarah Myers McGinty (College Board, 1997); *Multicultural Student's Guide to Colleges: What Every African American, Hispanic, and Native American Applicant Needs to Know About America's Top Schools* by Robert Mitchell (rev. ed., Noonday, 1996); and *100 Colleges Where Average Students Can Excel* by Joe Anne Adler (Macmillan, 1996), in addition to the popular annual editions of *America's 100 Best College Buys* (Juhn Culler & Sons), *The College Handbook* (College Board), and *Peterson's Competitive Colleges* (Peterson's Guides).

The Internet offers a plethora of college planning information as well. Consult *Netcollege: How to Get into the School of Your Dreams* by Michael Wolff (Wolff New Media, 1997). Connect directly to the home pages of colleges and universities from "Colleges & Universities—Worldwide Directory" at http://www. scholarstuff.com/colleges/colleges.htm; visit "CollegeNET" at http://www.collegenet.com/cgi-bin/ Webdriver?MIval=search_choices for scholarship and financial information; and check out "Apply to College" at http://www.applytocollege.com for virtual tours, links to admissions offices, and actual college applications.

Journalism/Sports Writing—Ben pays close attention to the wrestling write-ups in local and national newspapers. Sports writing requires a particular skill. Study sports writing in newspapers and magazines, many of which are also available online. Students can choose to cover a sporting event or interview players, coaches, or spectators. Publish or post the results. A helpful book is *How to Write a News Article* by Michael Kronenwetter (Franklin Watts, 1995).

Physical Education/Community Service—Teaching wrestling skills to younger kids is a tradition for the wrestlers at Sturbridge High School. This type of mentoring is a positive experience for all participants. Provide both sports and non-sports-related opportunities for teens to mentor in your community. Your students can participate in a variety of ways if they are provided with guidelines and adult supervision. Consider students helping adults with basic computer skills and Internet searching, being matched up with a "student at risk," tutoring in a specific subject area, being trained as a youth coach, and so on.

Writing/Songs/Poetry—Ben is enamored with a girl who works at a local gas station. He thinks, "She's somebody I could probably write a song about." (p. 7, hardback edition) Some students may already be writing song lyrics or poetry. Provide encouragement and resources, such as *Everything You Always Wanted to Know About Songwriting but Didn't Know Who to Ask* by Cliffie Stone and Joan Carol Stone (Showdown Enterprises, 1991); *Songwriting Wrongs & How to Right Them: Concrete Ways to Improve Your Songwriting and Make Your Songs More Marketable* by Pat Luboff and Pete Luboff (Writer's Digest Books, 1992); *The Craft of Lyric Writing* by Sheila Davis (Writer's Digest Books, 1985); and *Songwriting and the Creative Process: Suggestions and Starting Points for Songwriters* by Steve Gillette (Sing Out, 1995).

Takedown:

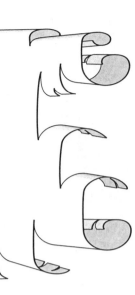

Great YA Authors for Guys

Bruce Brooks
Chris Crutcher
Terry Davis
Thomas Dygard
Robert Lipsyte
Chris Lynch
Harry Mazer
Walter Myers
Randy Powell
Todd Strasser
Rob Thomas
Paul Zindel

Takedown:

Wrestling As It Really Is!

Keith, Art. *Successful Wrestling: Coaches' Guide for Teaching Basic to Advanced Skills*

Lewin, Ted. *I Was a Teenage Professional Wrestler*

Martell, Bill. *An Illustrated Guide to Teaching Kids to Wrestle*

Mysnk, Mark. *Winning Wrestling Moves*

Savage, Jeff. *Wrestling Basics*

Wrestling: A Guide for Parents and Coaches

Takedown:

Wrestling Stories

Christopher, Matt. *Takedown*

Crutcher, Chris. *Athletic Shorts*

Killien, Christi. *Rusty Fertlanger, Lady's Man*

Klass, David. *Wrestling with Honor*

Marino, Tony. *Intergalactic Grudge Match*

Ogburn, Jacqueline K. *The Masked Maverick*

Wallace, Rich. *Riding Time*

Wallace, Rich. *Wrestling Sturbridge*

Wolff, Virginia Euwer
Make Lemonade

LC 92-41182. 1993. 200p. $15.95 (ISBN 0-8050-2228-7). Henry Holt and Company. 1994. 208p. $3.95pa. (ISBN 0-590-48141-X). Scholastic.

Genres: Contemporary realistic fiction, poetry

Themes: Teen mothers, babysitters, single-parent families, poverty, education, goals, choices, determination, love, friendship, despair, self-esteem, responsibility, sexual harassment, values, pride, homework, gang violence, homelessness, birth control, grammar, blank verse

Reading level: Sixth grade

Interest level: Seventh through twelfth grade

Reviews:
The Book Report. 12(3):49 November/December 1993 (Highly recommended)

Booklist. 89(19/20):1813 June 1/15, 1993. (Starred review)
Bulletin of the Center for Children's Books. 46(11):361 July/August 1993. (Recommended and starred)
Horn Book. 69(5):606–7 September/October 1993.
Kliatt Paperback and Audio Book Guide. 28(6):16 November 1994. (Starred review)
Publishers Weekly. 240(22):56 May 31, 1993.
School Library Journal. 39(7):103 July 1993. (Starred review)
Voice of Youth Advocates. 16(4):220 October 1993. (#4 quality, #3 popularity)

Author Information

An English teacher at a Hood River, Oregon, public high school since 1976, Virginia Euwer Wolff has taught every level from kindergarten to undergraduate school for nearly thirty years. She was born in Portland, Oregon, and attended Smith College and graduate schools in New York, North Carolina, and Oregon.

Wolff remembers her time as a young mother when she had to put her babies in "an old plastic-upholstered high chair from the Salvation Army that I could never get clean." Wolff says Jolly, Jilly, and Jeremy are products of that dirty high chair. She writes about issues that young people understand and says she agrees with Eudora Welty "that every story we write becomes our teacher."

Plot Summary

Teen mom Jolly needs a babysitter and posts an advertisement on a bulletin board at LaVaughn's high school. LaVaughn, earning money for college, takes the job and becomes intertwined in the struggling lives of Jolly and her two young children. LaVaughn's ambition and pragmatic attitude influence Jolly to take control of her own life and look at better choices for the future of her family.

Introducing the Book

This easy-to-read book has been a popular selection for reluctant young adult readers since its publication. The blank verse narrative with brief and (often) ungrammatical sentences is a powerful teenage voice. Introduce it with the booktalks and let readers experience it themselves. It's a must for every high school parenting and child development class.

Booktalks

On the Spot

There's an old saying: When life gives you lemons, make lemonade. The seventeen-year-old single mom with two kids in this book has had plenty of lemons. Can a fourteen-year-old babysitter help her turn lemons into lemonade?

With the Author's Words

Fourteen-year-old LaVaughn has answered an advertisement for a babysitting job.

> *I'm standing in their smelly apartment*
> *looking over the way things are going to be,*
> *me with these two small ones that I can already tell*
> *are leaking liquids everywhere.*
> *Jolly turns out to be 17. I could still say No*
> *just as quick as Jeremy did about my name.*
> *Then this Jolly she says, "I can't do it alone no longer,*
> *see, I'll get fired, it's a good job,*
> *I work for the factory, you work for me,*
> *Jilly and Jeremy can count on you being here,*
> *I can't do it alone." But while I'm listening*
> *and sneaking a look around at the mess*
> *and she repeats herself*
> *there's a surprise:*
> *Jeremy's hand is in my hand, he reached up for my fingers*
> *at the same time she says, "I can't do it alone"*
> *for her third time. (p. 7, hardback edition)*

Would you take this job? LaVaughn does, and it changes many lives, including her own.

Literature Extensions/Alternative Book Report Activities

Life Skills/Parenting—Statistically, teen parents do not grow up in families where good parenting skills are practiced. Teen parenting classes are an excellent way to help these young parents learn positive parenting behavior. Assemble a book collection to supplement teen parent programs or as a resource for those teens who are already parenting on their own.

Morning Glory Press, Inc. (6595 San Haroldo Way, Buena Park, CA 90620; telephone: 714-828-1998; fax: 714-828-2049) is devoted to publishing excellent books about issues concerning teen parents. Contact them for their complete list. Also consider the following books to help meet the needs of teen parents: *Fathers & Babies: How Babies Grow and What They Need from You, from Birth to 18 Months* (HarperPerennial, 1993) and *Fathers & Babies: How Babies Grow and What They Need from You, from 18 Months to Three Years of Age* (HarperPerennial, 1994), both by Jean Marzollo; *Living with Your Baby and Your Parents Under One Roof* by Carolyn Simpson (Rosen Publishing Group, 1996), and *Reality Check: Teenage Fathers Speak Out* by Margi Trapani (Rosen Publishing Group, 1997).

Literature/Reading Aloud/Teen Parents—It's easy to imagine that Jolly saw virtually no positive parenting skills modeled by her own parents. Most teen parents were rarely read to as children and do not understand the value of reading aloud to their own children and the connection to future school success. Model reading-aloud skills while helping to motivate teen parents to read to their own children. Careful selection of emotionally-charged, humorous, and topical picture books (or selected chapters from longer children's books) is the key to capturing the interest of teen parents. If a particular children's book appeals to a teen parent, that parent may be motivated to read aloud to their own child or children.

The following books have been read aloud to and enjoyed by teen parents: *Alexander and the Terrible, Horrible, No Good, Very Bad Day* by Judith Viorst (Atheneum, 1972); *All About Sam* by Lois Lowry (Houghton Mifflin, 1987); *A Couple of Kooks and Other Stories About Love* by Cynthia Rylant (Bantam, 1990); *How Many Days to America? A Thanksgiving Story* by Eve Bunting (Clarion Books, 1988); *Like Jake and Me* by Mavis Jukes (Alfred A. Knopf, 1984); *Piggybook* by Anthony Browne (Alfred A. Knopf,

1986); *We Are All in the Dumps with Jack and Guy: Two Nursery Rhymes with Pictures*, illustrated by Maurice Sendak (HarperCollins, 1993); *Broken Umbrellas* by Kate Spohn (Viking, 1994); *Cracker Jackson* by Betsy Byars (Viking, 1985); and *Faithful Elephants: A True Story of the Animals, People and War* by Yukio Tsuchiya (Houghton Mifflin, 1988). For others, see the "Read Aloud to Teens? Yes, with These Great Books!" bookmark.

Social Studies/Health—LaVaughn is a very responsible babysitter and depends on her mother and common sense to do a good job. Many teens who have little experience with younger children will consider babysitting an easy way to earn money. Help them out by developing a babysitting clinic and outlining responsibilities and procedures to follow in order to become a first-rate sitter. Include safety information as well as first aid and entertainment possibilities. Invite a health professional or EMT (emergency medical technician) to demonstrate and discuss CPR and the Heimlich maneuver. Bring in an early childhood specialist or children's librarian to present developmentally sound and safe activities, toys, and stories.

Read Aloud to Teens? Yes, with These Great Books!

Berger, Barbara. *Grandfather Twilight*

Bunting, Eve. *Smoky Night*

Bunting, Eve. *The Wall*

Fox, Mem. *Wilfrid Gordon McDonald Partridge*

Gallico, Paul. *The Snow Goose*

Garland, Sherry. *I Never Knew Your Name*

Innocenti, Roberto. *Rose Blanche*

Paulsen, Gary. *Nightjohn*

Prelutsky, Jack. *My Parents Think I'm Sleeping*

Prelutsky, Jack. *Somebody Big Has Been Here*

Scieszka, Jon. *The True Story of the Three Little Pigs*

Taylor, Clark. *The House That Crack Built*

Van Allsburg, Chris. *The Widow's Broom*

Viorst, Judith. *If I Were in Charge of the World and Other Worries*

Wild, Margaret. *Let the Celebrations Begin!*

Teen Parents —The Facts

Shirley Arthur's revised edition of *Surviving Teen Pregnancy: Your Choices, Dreams, and Decisions*

Eleanor H. Ayer's *Everything You Need to Know About Teen Fatherhood*

Karen Gravelle and Leslie Peterson's *Teenage Father* Jeanne Warren Lindsay and Sharon Githens Enright's *Books, Babies and School-Age Parents: How to Teach Pregnant and Parenting Teens to Succeed*

Jeanne Warren Lindsay's *Teenage Couples—Coping with Reality: Dealing with Money, In-Laws, Babies and Other Details of Daily Life*

Jean Marzollo's *Fathers & Babies: How Babies Grow and What They Need from You, from Birth to 18 Months*

Carolyn Simpson's *Living with Your Baby and Your Parents Under One Roof*

Margi Trapani's *Reality Check: Teenage Fathers Speak Out*

Teen Parents —Fiction

Benedict, Helen. *Bad Angel*

Christiansen, C. B. *I See the Moon*

Cole, Sheila. *What Kind of Love? Diary of a Pregnant Teen*

Doherty, Berlie. *Dear Nobody*

Klein, Norma. *No More Saturday Nights*

Reynolds, Marilyn. *But What About Me?*

Reynolds, Marilyn. *Detour for Emmy*

Reynolds, Marilyn. *Too Soon for Jeff*

Rodowsky, Colby. *Lucy Peale*

Thomas, Abigail. *An Actual Life: A Novel*

Waddell, Martin. *Tango's Baby*

Williams-Garcia, Rita. *Like Sisters on the Homefront*

Wolff, Virginia Euwer. *Make Lemonade*

Woodson, Jacqueline. *The Dear One*

Wurmfeld, Hope Herman. *Baby Blues*

Author/Title Index

Genres, Themes, and Activities Index

metaphors, 110
microbiology, 112
microorganisms, 113
microscopes, 6, 7, 112, 113
microscopic images, 113
middle age, 26, 75, 76
Middle East, 98
migrant labor, 32
migrant workers, 33
mind control, 50
miniatures, 15
misunderstanding, 26
mobs, 97
mock trials, 11
modern cities, 94
money, 17
monologues, 82
mothers and daughters, 26
mothers and sons, 88, 103
mountain climbing, 29
mourning, 82
movies, 29
moving, 88
multicultural, 3, 14, 17, 20, 29, 35, 47, 53, 56, 69, 79, 82, 85, 91, 97, 109, 124
murder, 23, 85
murder in schools, 86
music, 32
music, piano, 3
mutations, 50
mystery, 20, 23, 85, 106, 118

native cultures, 70
natural disasters, 72
neighborhoods, 79, 80, 82, 106
neighbors, 72
newspapers, 122
nonfiction, 23, 29, 38, 44, 94, 100, 112, 121
North Carolina, 56

obedience, 50
Olympics, 29, 30
opportunities, 17
oppression, 63
oral histories, 47, 56, 57
orphans, 6, 10, 63, 97
outlaws, 63

pain, 109
paleontology, 20
Palestine, 97
Palestinians and Jews, 98

panic, 72
the paranormal, 14
parasites, 112
parenting, 73, 103, 128
parents, 72
parodies, 60
passion, 91
peace, 35
peer pressure, 88, 106
peer relationships,
perspective, 44, 94
photography, 23, 112
physical development, 26, 121
physical education, 125
physical therapy, 109
physicians, 6
physics, 15, 44, 45
physiology, 15
picture books, 47, 94, 98
pigeons, 95
pirates, 10, 11
plays, 91
poaching, 63
poetry, 17, 18, 85, 110, 125, 127
pogroms, 97
point of view, 60, 82, 94
poison, 106
police and detectives, 24
police, 23
political oppression, 53
political refugees, 53
politics, 79
pollution, 50, 79, 118
popular culture, 83
postapartheid, 35
poverty, 56, 63, 127
power, 60
pranks, 26
pregnancy, 26
prejudice, 3, 56, 82, 91
pressure, 17
pride, 69, 127
prisons, 47
probation, 103
productivity, 82
professions, 44
prohibition, 79
property, 79
psychic phenomena, 14, 15
psychology, 15, 42, 110, 116, 122
puberty, 121
public housing, 79
public relations, 29